Dr. Roger Farr's
Think Reading

Think-Along Strategies for Reading Comprehension and Test Taking

Level **D**

Dr. Roger Farr
Elizabeth Haydel
Kimberly Munroe
Bruce Tone

RALLY!
EDUCATI●N

We're all about student success! ®

Acknowledgments

Senior Author: Dr. Roger Farr
Co-Authors: Elizabeth Haydel, Kimberly Munroe, Bruce Tone
Executive Editor: Amy Collins
Project Manager: Edward Nasello
Design Director: Jean-Paul Vest
Designer: Jan Jarvis, Willow Graphics
Cover Illustrator: Burgandy Beam

ISBN 978-1-4204-3471-2

408.MAQ

RALLY! EDUCATION
22 Railroad Avenue
Glen Head, NY 11545
(888) 99-RALLY

Contents

To the Teacher
Think Reading

What do good readers think about? They think about . . .

what they are reading.
what the words mean.
what the author is writing about.
what the places in a story look like.
what the people in a story are like.

This book will help students think about what they read.
The stories in this book have boxes with questions in them. These are spaces for students to write down what they are thinking *while they are reading*. This will help students think about what they read. Thinking about what they read will help students:

- enjoy reading,
- remember what they read, and
- answer questions about what they read.

This book will help students do better on tests.
To help students do better on tests, this book will ask them to:

Think When They Read
- read different stories about different people and things
- think along as they read

Think About the Question
- write answers to questions about what they read
- explain why they write the answers they do

Think When They Answer
- answer questions like the ones they see on tests

To the Teacher
Program Philosophy

RALLY! Education's *Think Reading: Think-Along Strategies for Reading Comprehension and Test Taking* has been developed to help students become strategic readers. Strategic readers are better able to comprehend and understand what they read.

The unique feature of this series of books is that students are taught to apply reading strategies to the kinds of reading selections and questions they encounter on standardized tests.

However, the series is not designed merely to make your students better test takers. Rather, the series is designed to help your students become better readers who will apply their better reading strategies to assessments they encounter. The philosophy behind *Think Reading* is that if students know how to think along as they read, they will achieve better results when taking tests.

By **thinking along** while they read passages and answer test items, students will learn to read the passages more effectively. When you use this series with your students, you will help them become better readers. Not coincidentally, you will also help them to improve their performance on tests that emphasize reading comprehension.

RALLY! Education's *Think Reading* series is designed to give students opportunities to:

- think and make meaning while they read.
- use reading strategies to become better comprehenders.
- practice thinking strategies that improve performance on reading comprehension tests.
- read a variety of texts like those they will encounter in testing situations.
- answer a variety of comprehension questions like those they will encounter in testing situations.
- become familiar with common test formats and directions.

The activities in this book can be integrated easily into your regular classroom instruction. The Student Edition is easy to use. The Teacher's Guide gives clear suggestions for **scaffolded instruction** that will allow students to work more and more independently as they progress through the Student Edition.

To the Teacher

Features of the Student Edition

ORGANIZATION

The Student Edition includes three sections:

• **Modeled Instruction:** Test-taking strategies for reading comprehension are introduced in this unit. Students apply the strategies they learn to passages that focus on functional information, fiction, and nonfiction. Transparencies are provided for each passage and related question.

• **Guided Practice:** In this section, students are given guided practice in thinking about:
1) what they read.
2) how they answer questions in test-taking situations.

• **Independent Practice:** In the last section, students are given opportunities for independent practice. Students read functional, fiction, and nonfiction passages and answer multiple-choice and open-ended questions based on each passage.

THEMES

Several themes of interest to students connect the passages in each section of this book. Before students read thematically connected passages, ask them to read the theme page.

• **Theme 1 (Modeled Instruction):** The theme page and the corresponding think-along question can be read and completed as a shared read-aloud activity.

• **Themes 2, 3, & 4 (Guided Practice):** Ask students to read each theme page and answer the think-along question independently. Then discuss students' varied responses.

• **Themes 5, 6, & 7 (Independent Practice):** The themes are summarized briefly and unaccompanied by think-along questions. Students should read these summaries independently as they would in a testing situation.

An **extended-response** question appears at the end of each theme. After students have read all passages of a theme, ask them to answer the extended-response question.

The themes in Level D are summarized in the chart below.

Unit	Page	Theme	Topic
Modeled Instruction	11	Helping Hands	Ways that people help others and help to improve the places where they live
Guided Practice	39	Take Me to The Game	The importance of sport in people's lives
	65	What Makes Me, Me?	How science and experience help to shape who we are
	91	Flights of Discovery	The realities and possibilities created by flight
Independent Practice	119	Holidays and Celebrations	The importance of special holidays and celebrations in people's lives
	133	Ancient Animals	What kinds of animals used to walk the earth and how we know about them
	147	Learning from Each Other	How people from different parts of the world can learn from each other

To the Teacher
Scope and Sequence

Objective	Reading Skills and Strategies	Grade 4
Understanding Literal Meanings	Recall Facts and Details	●
	Identify Sequence	●
Interpreting and Extending Meaning	Use Context Clues to Understand Words and Phrases	●
	Identify Main Idea	●
	Predict Outcomes	●
	Compare and Contrast	●
	Recognize Cause and Effect	●
	Make Inferences and Draw Conclusions	●
	Identify and Interpret Figurative Language	●
	Identify Story Elements: Character, Plot, and Setting	●
	Identify Story Elements: Theme	●
	Identify Tone and Mood	
Analyzing Text	Recognize and Evaluate Text Organization	●
	Distinguish between Fantasy and Reality	●
	Distinguish Fact from Opinion	
	Identify Author's/Text's Purpose and Audience	●
	Analyze Author's Point of View	●
	Identify and Analyze Author's Techniques	●
	Identify Point of View	
Applying Strategies	Summarize	●
	Identify Genres and Types of Passages	●
	Use Research and Reference Skills	●
	Adjust Reading for Different Purposes	●
	Distinguish between Relevant and Irrelevant Information	
	Use Details to Support Conclusions	

These four reading strategies represent individualized strategies that students use to comprehend while reading. They are introduced through think-along questions but not assessed by test items.

Individualized Thinking Strategies	Connect Personal Experiences	●
	Visualize	●
	Generate Questions	●
	Apply Prior Knowledge	●

To the Student
Test-Taking Tips

Here are some ideas that can help you do better on any test you take.

1. **Know what you need to do.**
Make sure you understand what you need to do. Listen to, read, and think about the directions. Ask questions about directions you do not understand.

2. **Read carefully.**
Read every story carefully. Think about the important ideas. Read the questions carefully. Think about what each question is asking.

3. **Read the story first.**
Read and think about the story first. Then read and answer the questions about that story. Don't look at the questions before you read the story.

4. **Think about your answers.**
Before you look at the answer choices for a question, think about the answer. Choose the answer that is the most like your answer.

5. **Guess if you have to.**
If you do not know the answer, it is okay to guess. But before you guess, cross out any answer choices you know are wrong. This will make it easier to guess the right answer.

6. **Write clearly.**
If you write an answer to a question, make sure you write clearly. Make sure the person who reads your answer can understand what you mean. Write neatly. Read over your answer. Make sure it answers the question.

7. **Write correctly.**
Use sentences. Start your sentences with uppercase letters. Read over your answer. Make sure it does not have mistakes.

8. **Use your time well.**
If you don't know the answer to a question, go to the next question. Come back to any hard questions at the end.

9. **Be good to yourself.**
Get a good night's sleep the night before the test. Eat a good breakfast before you take the test.

10. **Know that you can do well!**
A test is a chance for you to show what you know. You can do it!

Modeled Instruction
We Lead You

Theme 1: Helping Hands

Local Activities	Functional/Everyday
The Boy Who Saved a Village	Fiction
Making Your World Better	Nonfiction

The Think Reading Strategy for Reading Comprehension and Test Taking

In this book, you will learn how to use the *Think Reading* **Strategy for Reading Comprehension and Test Taking**. There are three steps you will follow. The first step is completed when reading each passage. The second and third steps are completed when answering questions about each passage.

Reading the Passages

Think When You Read

You will read each passage. As you read, you will ask yourself questions about the passage. This will help you to better understand the passage and remember important details.

Answering the Questions

After you have read each passage, you will answer questions about the passage. You will see the same set of questions twice.

Think About the Question

Read questions *without the multiple-choice answers.* Think about what each question is asking you. Write what you think the correct answer is. Explain why you think this is the answer.

Think When You Answer

Now answer *the same questions again*. This time the questions will appear as they would on a test. For multiple-choice questions, you will be given four possible answers to choose from. Look back at what you wrote on the "Think About the Question" pages. This will help you answer each question correctly.

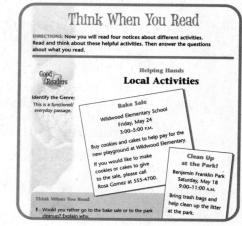

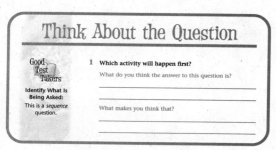

Introduction to Theme 1:
Helping Hands

There are many ways we can help others and make the place where we live a better place to be. Sometimes helping can be something as small as smiling and saying hello to a neighbor. Sometimes helping can be something bigger, like planting a garden in your town or planning a dinner to feed hungry people.

Now you will read three stories. These stories tell something about ways that people can help or have helped others. As you read, think about what you could do to make the world a better place.

Think When You Read

1 What could you do to help make the place where you live a better place to be?

_____

_____

Think When You Read

DIRECTIONS: Now you will read four notices about different activities. Read and think about these helpful activities. Then answer the questions about what you read.

Good Readers

Identify the Genre:
This is a *functional/ everyday* passage.

Helping Hands
Local Activities

Bake Sale

Wildwood Elementary School
Friday, May 24
3:00–5:00 P.M.

Buy cookies and cakes to help pay for the new playground at Wildwood Elementary.

If you would like to make cookies or cakes to give to the sale, please call Rosa Gomez at 555-4700.

Clean Up at the Park!

Benjamin Franklin Park
Saturday, May 18
9:00–11:00 A.M.

Bring trash bags and help clean up the litter at the park.

Think When You Read

1 Would you rather go to the bake sale or to the park cleanup? Explain why.

_____

_____

_____

Young People Needed

to help at the
Centerville Senior Citizen's Home
Spring Fair

Saturday, June 1

People ages 9–17 who are good at telling stories, singing, or playing music are asked to come and perform.

Call Emma Harris at 555-2000 to learn more.

Help make an older person's day brighter!

Garden Days

Southside Elementary School
Saturday, May 25 and Sunday, May 26
9:00 A.M. to noon both days

Help make the Southside Schoolyard more beautiful. Helpers needed to plant plants, weed, and cut the grass at Southside Elementary.

Sponsored by J. Graeter's Garden Supply Store

Think When You Read

2 Which of these activities do you think more people would take part in? Tell why.

_____

_____

_____

THINK READING STRATEGY FOR TEST TAKING

You will now answer questions about the passage you just read. You will answer the same questions twice. First, answer the questions without knowing the answer choices.

Think About the Question: Write what you think the answer is.
Write what made you think that.

Think About the Question

Good Test Takers

Identify What Is Being Asked:

This is a *sequence* question.

1 Which activity will happen first?

What do you think the answer to this question is?

_____

_____

What makes you think that?

_____

_____

Good Test Takers

Identify What Is Being Asked:

This is a *facts and details* question.

2 Whom should you call if you want to give cookies to the bake sale?

What do you think the answer to this question is?

_____

_____

What makes you think that?

_____

_____

3 **These activities mostly help**

What do you think the answer to this question is?

_____

_____

What makes you think that?

_____

_____

Identify What Is Being Asked:

This is an _inferences and conclusions_ question.

4 **Where would these notices probably appear?**

What do you think the answer to this question is?

_____

_____

What makes you think that?

_____

_____

Identify What Is Being Asked:

This is a _genres and types of passages_ question.

5 **Lydia Lee is 18 years old. She likes to do community activities on Saturdays and Sundays. Which activities can she do? Explain why.**

What do you think the answer to this question is?

_____

_____

What makes you think that?

_____

_____

Identify What Is Being Asked:

This is an _inferences and conclusions_ question.

THINK READING STRATEGY FOR TEST TAKING

You will now answer the same questions again. This time, answer choices will be provided for questions 1–4 (just as they would on a test). Choose the <u>best</u> possible answer to each question.

Think When You Answer: Choose your answer from the multiple-choice responses. Write why you chose that answer.

Think When You Answer

Good Test Takers

Eliminate Choices and Choose the Best Answer.

1 **Which activity will happen first?**

Ⓐ   the park cleanup

Ⓑ   the bake sale

Ⓒ   the senior citizen fair

Ⓓ   the garden days

Why did you choose your answer?

_____

_____

2 **Whom should you call if you want to give cookies to the bake sale?**

Ⓐ Benjamin Franklin

Ⓑ Rosa Gomez

Ⓒ Emma Harris

Ⓓ J. Graeter

Why did you choose your answer?

_____

_____

3 **These activities mostly help**

Ⓐ animals and people

Ⓑ people and the earth

Ⓒ young and sick people

Ⓓ old and hungry people

Why did you choose your answer?

_____

_____

Good Test Takers

Eliminate Choices and Choose the Best Answer.

4 **Where would these notices probably appear?**

Ⓐ in a telephone book

Ⓑ in a magazine for children

Ⓒ in a magazine about gardening

Ⓓ on a board in a grocery store

> Why did you choose your answer?
>
> _____
>
> _____
>
> _____

THINK READING STRATEGY FOR TEST TAKING

Question 5 is <u>not</u> a multiple-choice question. Read the question again and the answer that is given. Write about how your answer on page 15 was the same as this answer. Or write how it was different from this answer.

Good Test Takers

Support Answers with Facts and Details.

5 Lydia Lee is 18 years old. She likes to do community activities on Saturdays and Sundays. Which activities can she do? Explain why.

Answer: *She can help clean the park and work in the schoolyard garden because those events happen on the weekend, but she is too old to be a volunteer at the senior citizen fair.*

> How is this answer the same as or different from your answer?
>
> _____
>
> _____
>
> _____

18

Think When You Read

DIRECTIONS: Here is an old Japanese story about a boy named Yuuki who saves the people of his village. Read and think about the story. Then answer the questions about the story.

Helping Hands

The Boy Who Saved a Village

Long ago on an island in Japan, there lived a boy named Yuuki. Like the other children in his village, Yuuki helped his family grow rice. He liked to run and climb. And, he loved nature. He spent many hours listening to his grandfather tell stories about the power of the ocean and the earth.

One day, Yuuki climbed the mountain behind his village. From the mountaintop, Yuuki saw the whole village and the deep blue ocean spread out below him. The people in the village were preparing for a festival to celebrate the bountiful harvest of the rice crop. They had grown a lot of rice that year and would have food to last through the coming winter. The rice crop lay in golden stacks drying on the side of the mountain.

©Razvanjp/dreamstime.com

Good Readers

Identify the Genre:
This is a *fiction* passage.

Think When You Read

1 How do you think the people felt as they got ready for the festival?

_____

_____

_____

After starting down the mountain, Yuuki stopped when he felt the ground move. The movement was not unusual because there were often small earthquakes where Yuuki lived. This time, though, the ground moved in a different way, in a long, slow, rolling motion. Yuuki looked down at the ocean and saw the water moving quickly away from the village. Suddenly, the sandy beach stretched almost as far as Yuuki could see. He saw people running onto the beach, chasing the water.

Think When You Read

2 What do you think is going to happen?

_____

_____

_____

Yuuki remembered a story his grandfather had told him about how the ocean could bring terrible, giant waves onto the island. Before these terrible waves came, the ocean suddenly moved away from the shore. Yuuki ran to tell the others.

Yuuki did not know what to do. The people did not believe him. He ran up the mountain. He took a stick and lit it on fire. He lit the stacks of rice. As the orange flames of the fire grew higher, the people on the beach smelled the smoke. They saw the fire.

All of the people ran up the mountain to try to put out the fire. "Yuuki is crazy!" they screamed, when they realized he had lit the fire.

But, just then, the ocean rose up and formed a great, dark wall of water that came crashing down over the beach and the village. The wave almost reached the top of the mountain where the people of the village stood. It crashed over the village and the beach below.

The people were silent, as they looked down at their ruined village and the empty fields where their rice had been. Then all at once they turned to look at Yuuki. "You saved us all!" they cried. "We cannot celebrate the great harvest of our rice tonight, but we can celebrate our lives. Tonight we will have a party for Yuuki, who saved us from the terrible wave."

Think When You Read

3 How would you feel if you were Yuuki?

_____

_____

_____

THINK READING STRATEGY FOR TEST TAKING

You will now answer questions about the passage you just read. You will answer the same questions twice. First, answer the questions without knowing the answer choices.

Think About the Question: Write what you think the answer is.
Write what made you think that.

Think About the Question

Good Test Takers

Identify What Is Being Asked:

This is a *main idea* question.

1 **What is this story mostly about?**

What do you think the answer to this question is?

_____

_____

What makes you think that?

_____

_____

Good Test Takers

Identify What Is Being Asked:

This is an *inferences and conclusions* question.

2 **The best way to describe Yuuki is to say that he is a boy who**

What do you think the answer to this question is?

_____

_____

What makes you think that?

_____

_____

3 **The next time the ocean moves quickly away from the beach, the people in the village will probably**

What do you think the answer to this question is?

_____

_____

What makes you think that?

_____

_____

Good Test Takers

Identify What Is Being Asked:

This is a *prediction* question.

4 **This story is most like a**

What do you think the answer to this question is?

_____

_____

What makes you think that?

_____

_____

Good Test Takers

Identify What Is Being Asked:

This is a *genres and types of passages* question.

5 **Why did Yuuki light the rice stacks on fire?**

What do you think the answer to this question is?

_____

_____

What makes you think that?

_____

_____

Good Test Takers

Identify What Is Being Asked:

This is a *cause and effect* question.

THINK READING STRATEGY FOR TEST TAKING

You will now answer the same questions again. This time, answer choices will be provided for questions 1–4 (just as they would on a test). Choose the **best** possible answer to each question.

Think When You Answer: Choose your answer from the multiple-choice responses. Write why you chose that answer.

Think When You Answer

Good Test Takers

Eliminate Choices and Choose the Best Answer.

1 **What is this story mostly about?**

Ⓐ a tall mountain

Ⓑ a day at the beach

Ⓒ a boy and a giant wave

Ⓓ a boy and his grandfather

Why did you choose your answer?

_____

_____

_____

2 **The best way to describe Yuuki is to say that he is a boy who**

Ⓐ did not think about others

Ⓑ did not remember things

Ⓒ was quiet and shy

Ⓓ was brave and wise

Why did you choose your answer?

_____

_____

_____

3 **The next time the ocean moves quickly away from the beach, the people in the village will probably**

Ⓐ go to the beach to pick up fish

Ⓑ stay in the village for a party

Ⓒ wait for Yuuki's help

Ⓓ run to the top of the mountain

Why did you choose your answer?

_____

_____

_____

Good Test Takers

Eliminate Choices and Choose the Best Answer.

4 **This story is most like a**

Ⓐ mystery

Ⓑ science book

Ⓒ folktale

Ⓓ fairy tale

Why did you choose your answer?

_____

_____

THINK READING STRATEGY FOR TEST TAKING

Question 5 is <u>not</u> a multiple-choice question. Read the question again and the answer that is given. Write about how your answer on page 23 was the same as this answer. Or write how it was different from this answer.

Good Test Takers

Support Answers with Facts and Details.

5 **Why did Yuuki light the rice stacks on fire?**

Answer: *He wanted the villagers to run up the mountain to safety.*

How is this answer the same as or different from your answer?

_____

_____

_____

Think When You Read

DIRECTIONS: Now you will learn more about volunteers. Volunteers are people who work for free to help make life better for people around them. Think about what you read and then answer the questions.

Helping Hands

Making Your World Better

Identify the Genre:
This is a *nonfiction* passage.

Are there things you would like to do to make your town a better place to live? Would you like to help other people? Do you care about animals?

You might wonder how you can help and whether one young person can make a difference. Yes, one young person can. Being a volunteer is one way to make a difference. Volunteers are people who work for free to help other people, animals, or the earth. There are many ways that volunteers help.

Volunteers improve people's lives in many different ways. Some volunteers go to hospitals to visit sick children or older people. Others collect cans of food to <u>donate</u> to hungry people.

©*iStockphoto.com/annedde*

Think When You Read

1 What could you do to make a difference?

_____

_____

_____

In your town, are there people from other countries who do not yet speak English well? Volunteers work with these people to help teach them English.

Some volunteers work with animals. They collect food or toys to take to animal shelters, places that keep lost cats and dogs. Volunteers help find good homes for cats and dogs that need homes. Feeding birds or setting up birdbaths in backyards or schoolyards are other ways that volunteers can help animals.

Think When You Read

2 Can you think of additional ways that people could help other people and animals?

_____

_____

_____

Young people who volunteer can also work to help the earth by picking up trash or by recycling. Recycling means collecting things that can be made into different things. Paper, cans, and glass bottles can all be used to make new things. Young people can help the earth by not throwing paper, cans, or glass away and instead taking these things to a place where they can be recycled.

What would you like to do to make a difference?

Think When You Read

3 Tell about a volunteer you know about who has made a difference.

_____

_____

_____

THINK READING STRATEGY FOR TEST TAKING

You will now answer questions about the passage you just read. You will answer the same questions twice. First, answer the questions without knowing the answer choices.

Think About the Question: Write what you think the answer is.
Write what made you think that.

Think About the Question

Good Test Takers

Identify What Is Being Asked:

This is a *main idea* question.

1 **What is another good name for this story?**

What do you think the answer to this question is?

_____

_____

What makes you think that?

_____

_____

Good Test Takers

Identify What Is Being Asked:

This is an *inferences and conclusions* question.

2 **One example of a volunteer is a person who**

What do you think the answer to this question is?

_____

_____

What makes you think that?

_____

_____

3 **In this story, to <u>donate</u> means to**

What do you think the answer to this question is?

_____

_____

What makes you think that?

_____

_____

Good Test Takers

Identify What Is Being Asked:

This is a *words and phrases* question.

4 **To answer Question 3, what part of the story should you read?**

What do you think the answer to this question is?

_____

_____

What makes you think that?

_____

_____

Good Test Takers

Identify What Is Being Asked:

This is a *reading for different purposes* question.

5 **Why was this story written?**

What do you think the answer to this question is?

_____

_____

What makes you think that?

_____

_____

Good Test Takers

Identify What Is Being Asked:

This is an *author's purpose* question.

THINK READING STRATEGY FOR TEST TAKING

You will now answer the same questions again. This time, answer choices will be provided for questions 1–4 (just as they would on a test). Choose the <u>best</u> possible answer to each question.

Think When You Answer: Choose your answer from the multiple-choice responses. Write why you chose that answer.

Think When You Answer

Good Test Takers

Eliminate Choices and Choose the Best Answer.

1   **What is another good name for this story?**

Ⓐ "Animals and People"

Ⓑ "Clean Up the Earth!"

Ⓒ "Helpful Volunteers"

Ⓓ "How to Help the Sick"

Why did you choose your answer?

_____

_____

_____

2 **One example of a volunteer is a person who**

Ⓐ plays baseball and soccer

Ⓑ works at a movie theatre

Ⓒ cooks dinner for his or her family

Ⓓ helps at the library by reading to children

Why did you choose your answer?

_____

_____

_____

3 **In this story, to <u>donate</u> means to**

Ⓐ give to

Ⓑ take from

Ⓒ talk to

Ⓓ buy from

Why did you choose your answer?

_____

_____

_____

Good Test Takers

Eliminate Choices and Choose the Best Answer.

4 To answer Question 3, what part of the story should you read?

Ⓐ the title of the story

Ⓑ the first line of each paragraph

Ⓒ the last paragraph

Ⓓ the part where you see the word <u>donate</u>

> Why did you choose your answer?
>
> _____
>
> _____
>
> _____

THINK READING STRATEGY FOR TEST TAKING

Question 5 is <u>not</u> a multiple-choice question. Read the question again and the answer that is given. Write about how your answer on page 31 was the same as this answer. Or write how it was different from this answer.

Good Test Takers

Support Answers with Facts and Details.

5 Why was this story written?

Answer: *This story was written to tell young people about what they can do to help.*

> How is this answer the same as or different from your answer?
>
> _____
>
> _____
>
> _____

Theme Question

DIRECTIONS: The extended-response question below requires you to think about more than one of the passages you have just read. Read the question carefully and write your answer in the space provided. Use complete sentences, correct punctuation, and proper grammar. Be sure to answer each part of the question.

EXTENDED-RESPONSE QUESTION
THEME 1: HELPING HANDS

Of the helpful activities that you have just read about, which would you like to do most? Why? Explain how these activities would help make the world a better place.

Use details from the passages you have just read to support your answer.

_____

_____

_____

_____

_____

_____

_____

_____

_____

_____

_____

_____

_____

_____

Guided Practice
We Guide You

Theme 2: Take Me to the Game

A Ticket to the Game	Functional/Everyday
From Soccer to Football	Fiction
The Special Olympics	Nonfiction

Theme 3: What Makes Me, Me?

Why Are You, You?	Functional/Everyday
Chopsticks and Forks	Fiction
Look at My Genes!	Nonfiction

Theme 4: Flights of Discovery

How Does It Fly?	Functional/Everyday
Not So Different After All	Fiction
Ellen Ochoa: Astronaut	Nonfiction

Think Reading Strategy Review

Remember to use the *Think Reading* **Strategy for Reading Comprehension and Test Taking**. There are three steps you must follow. The first step is completed when reading each passage. The second and third steps are completed when answering questions about each passage.

Reading the Passages

Think When You Read

As you read each passage, ask yourself questions. This will help you to better understand the passage and remember important details.

Answering the Questions

After you have read each passage, answer questions about the passage. You will see the same set of questions twice.

Think About the Question

Read questions *without the multiple-choice answers*. Think about what each question is asking you. Write what you think the correct answer is. Explain why you think this is the answer.

Think When You Answer

Answer *the same questions again*. This time the questions appear as they would on a test. There are four answer choices for each multiple-choice question. Look back at what you wrote on the "Think About the Question" pages. This will help you answer each question correctly.

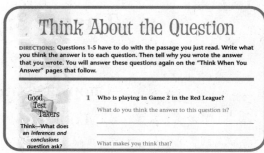

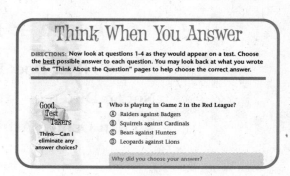

Introduction to Theme 2:

Take Me to the Game

People around the world enjoy playing and watching games and sports. Some people like games and sports because they like the feelings that come from playing and winning. Others enjoy the ways that games and sports make them feel healthy and good about themselves.

Now you will read three stories. These stories tell something about games and sports. As you read, think about what games and sports you like to play and why.

Think When You Read

1 What games and sports do you like to play? Why?

_____

_____

_____

Think When You Read

DIRECTIONS: Now you will read a schedule for a basketball tournament and a ticket to one of the games. Read and think about what you read. Then answer the questions about what you read.

Think—What do I think this passage will be about?

Take Me to the Game
A Ticket to the Game

2003 Girls' Basketball Tournament Schedule

Round One

Red League

Game 1

Who: Raiders against Badgers

Where: Albany High School Gym

Date: March 15, 2003

Time: 3:00 P.M.

Game 2

Who: Squirrels against Cardinals

Where: Albany High School Gym

Date: March 15, 2003

Time: 5:00 P.M.

Blue League

Game 1

Who: Bears against Hunters

Where: Franklin Middle School Gym

Date: March 15, 2003

Time: 3:00 P.M.

Game 2

Who: Leopards against Lions

Where: Franklin Middle School Gym

Date: March 15, 2003

Time: 5:00 P.M.

Think When You Read

1 Who do you think might be interested in reading this schedule?

_____

_____

_____

Ticket
for the 2003 Girls' Basketball Tournament

Date:	March 15
Location:	Franklin Middle School Gym
Time:	5:00 P.M.
Row:	12
Seat:	15

©*Katseyephoto/dreamstime.com*

Think When You Read

2 Would you like to go to a basketball game? Tell why or why not.

_____

_____

_____

Think About the Question

DIRECTIONS: Questions 1–5 have to do with the passage you just read. Write what you think the answer is to each question. Then tell why you wrote the answer that you wrote. You will answer these questions again on the "Think When You Answer" pages that follow.

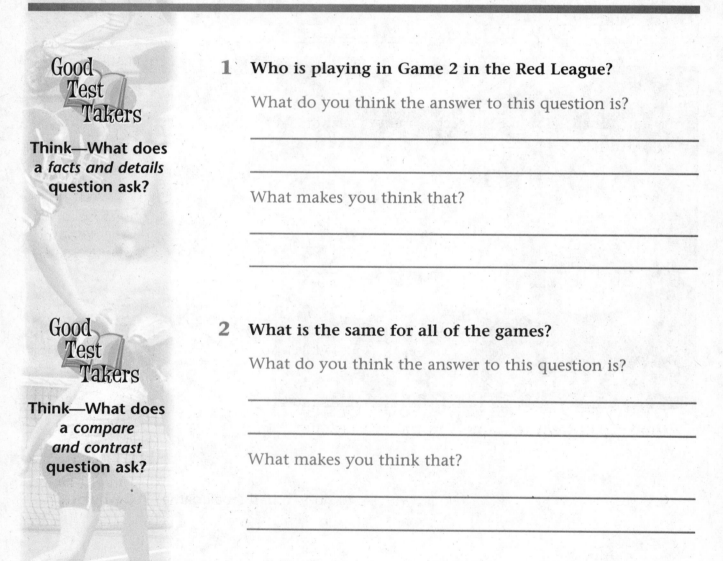

Good Test Takers

Think—What does a *facts and details* question ask?

1 **Who is playing in Game 2 in the Red League?**

What do you think the answer to this question is?

_____

_____

What makes you think that?

_____

_____

Good Test Takers

Think—What does a *compare and contrast* question ask?

2 **What is the same for all of the games?**

What do you think the answer to this question is?

_____

_____

What makes you think that?

_____

_____

3 **Which game is the ticket for?**

What do you think the answer to this question is?

_____

_____

What makes you think that?

_____

_____

_____

Good Test Takers

Think—What does an *inferences and conclusions* question ask?

4 **What information on the ticket helped you answer Question 3?**

What do you think the answer to this question is?

_____

_____

What makes you think that?

_____

_____

_____

Good Test Takers

Think—What does a *reading for different purposes* question ask?

5 **What would the ticket list as the date, location, and time if you went to Game 1 in the Red League?**

What do you think the answer to this question is?

_____

_____

What makes you think that?

_____

_____

_____

Good Test Takers

Think—What does a *prediction* question ask?

Think When You Answer

DIRECTIONS: Now look at questions 1–4 as they would appear on a test. Choose the <u>best</u> possible answer to each question. You may look back at what you wrote on the "Think About the Question" pages to help choose the correct answer.

Good Test Takers

Think—Can I eliminate any answer choices?

1 **Who is playing in Game 2 in the Red League?**

Ⓐ Raiders against Badgers

Ⓑ Squirrels against Cardinals

Ⓒ Bears against Hunters

Ⓓ Leopards against Lions

Why did you choose your answer?

_____

_____

_____

2 What is the same for all of the games?

Ⓐ the time they are played

Ⓑ the place they are played

Ⓒ the date they are played

Ⓓ the teams that are playing

Why did you choose your answer?

_____

_____

_____

3 Which game is the ticket for?

Ⓐ Game 1 in the Red League

Ⓑ Game 2 in the Red League

Ⓒ Game 1 in the Blue League

Ⓓ Game 2 in the Blue League

Why did you choose your answer?

_____

_____

_____

Good Test Takers

Think—Can I eliminate any answer choices?

4 **What information on the ticket helped you answer Question 3?**

Ⓐ Date

Ⓑ Location

Ⓒ Row

Ⓓ Seat

> **Why did you choose your answer?**
>
> _____
>
> _____

DIRECTIONS: Read question 5 again and the answer that is given. Then write about how your answer was the same as this answer. Or write how it was different from this answer. You will need to look back at what you wrote on the "Think About the Question" pages.

Good Test Takers

Think—What facts and details support my answer?

5 **What would the ticket list as the date, location, and time if you went to Game 1 in the Red League?**

Answer: *The ticket would list March 15, Albany High School Gym, and 3:00 P.M.*

> **How is this answer the same as or different from your answer?**
>
> _____
>
> _____

46

Think When You Read

DIRECTIONS: Here is a story about a Brazilian boy named Arlindo who worries that he will miss his friends and playing soccer when he moves to the United States. Read the story and then answer the questions.

Take Me to the Game
From Soccer to Football

Arlindo looked out the window of the car as it passed a field of boys playing soccer.

"What's bothering you?" asked his mother.

"I'm going to miss playing soccer. I'm going to miss all my friends here in Brazil, too," said Arlindo. "What if I don't make friends in Michigan?"

"You'll make friends in no time at all," said his mother, looking more confident than Arlindo felt.

Arlindo was still anxious. He'd lived in Brazil all his life.

Arlindo and his family arrived in Flint, Michigan, a couple of weeks before school was supposed to start.

That weekend, Arlindo and his father kicked a soccer ball at the park. Arlindo loved soccer. It was his favorite sport.

"I miss soccer, Dad," said Arlindo. "Do kids play soccer here?"

Good Readers

Think—What do I think this passage will be about?

Think When You Read

1 How would you feel about moving to a new place?

_____

_____

_____

©iStockphoto.com/Jim Kolaczko

"I'm certain they do, and with school about to start, you'll be on the team and making friends before you know it," said his father.

One week later Arlindo started school. He hoped Dad was right about making new friends. Arlindo's first class was gym. He was glad. This gave him a chance to find out about the soccer team right away.

As he waited for gym class to begin, he turned to a boy beside him and said, "Hi, my name is Arlindo. Do you play soccer at this school?"

"My name is Adam. Soccer? No, we don't play soccer," said Adam.

Just then Mrs. Hamilton, the gym teacher, walked in.

"Today we're going to learn about one of the most popular sports in the U.S.," said Mrs. Hamilton. "Football."

Arlindo had seen football but had never played. The class spent the first day throwing and catching the ball. Arlindo was awful. In soccer, you use your feet, not your hands. Only the goalie uses his hands in soccer, and Arlindo never played goalie.

When Mrs. Hamilton asked two students to select team members for a practice game, Arlindo was picked last.

Think When You Read

2 Arlindo likes to play soccer. What do you like to do? Why?

_____

_____

_____

"How was your first day at school?" asked his mother and father when he came home.

"Rotten," said Arlindo, as he slammed the door and went into his room.

The next day, Arlindo didn't want to go to school, and he didn't want to play football.

"Today we're going to practice a different part of football," said Mrs. Hamilton. "Kicking."

Arlindo's eyes lit up. "Kicking," he thought. "I know how to kick!"

Mrs. Hamilton showed the class how to kick a football and then had students practice. Arlindo could kick the ball twice as far as anyone else. His classmates stopped to watch him kick.

This time when Mrs. Hamilton assigned two students to select teams for a practice game, Arlindo was chosen first.

"Wow!" said Adam. "It's amazing how far you can kick the ball. Will you show me how to kick like that?"

"I'd love to," said Arlindo. "I can also teach you how to kick a soccer ball."

"Awesome," said Adam.

"How was your second day of school?" asked his mother and father when Arlindo came home.

"Awesome," said Arlindo.

> **Think When You Read**
>
> **3** Have you ever made a friend while playing a sport or doing another activity? Tell something about that time.
>
> _____
>
> _____
>
> _____

Think About the Question

DIRECTIONS: Questions 1–5 have to do with the passage you just read. Write what you think the answer is to each question. Then tell why you wrote the answer that you wrote. You will answer these questions again on the "Think When You Answer" pages that follow.

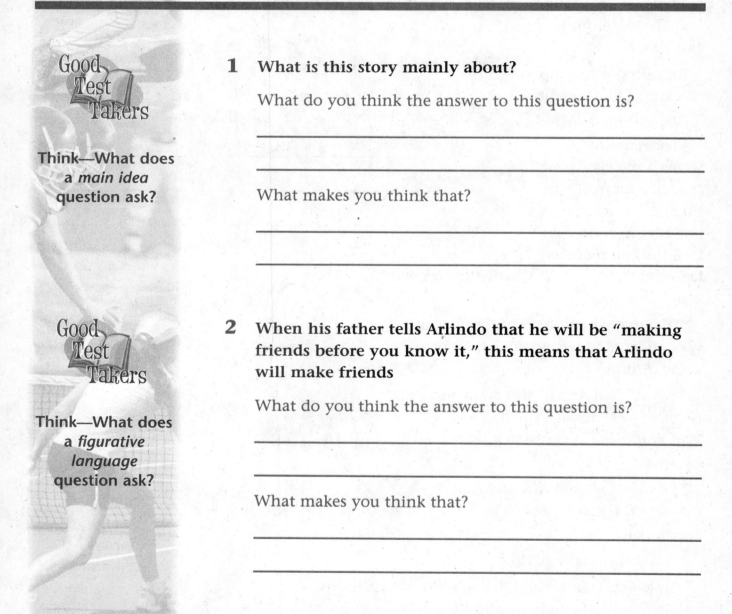

Good Test Takers

Think—What does *a main idea* question ask?

1 What is this story mainly about?

What do you think the answer to this question is?

_____

_____

What makes you think that?

_____

_____

Good Test Takers

Think—What does a *figurative language* question ask?

2 When his father tells Arlindo that he will be "making friends before you know it," this means that Arlindo will make friends

What do you think the answer to this question is?

_____

_____

What makes you think that?

_____

_____

3 **At the end of the story, Arlindo probably feels**

What do you think the answer to this question is?

_____

_____

What makes you think that?

_____

_____

4 **What detail from the story best shows the answer to Question 3?**

What do you think the answer to this question is?

_____

_____

What makes you think that?

_____

_____

5 **Why does Arlindo say his second day at school was "awesome"?**

What do you think the answer to this question is?

_____

_____

What makes you think that?

_____

_____

Think When You Answer

DIRECTIONS: Now look at questions 1–4 as they would appear on a test. Choose the <u>best</u> possible answer to each question. You may look back at what you wrote on the "Think About the Question" pages to help choose the correct answer.

Good
Test
Takers

Think—Can I eliminate any answer choices?

1 **What is this story mainly about?**

Ⓐ how Brazil is different from the United States

Ⓑ how soccer is different from football

Ⓒ how to learn to play football

Ⓓ how Arlindo learns football and makes friends

Why did you choose your answer?

_____

_____

_____

2 **When his father tells Arlindo that he will be "making friends before you know it," this means that Arlindo will make friends**

Ⓐ without knowing

Ⓑ quickly and easily

Ⓒ over time

Ⓓ like those he had in Brazil

Why did you choose your answer?

_____

_____

_____

3 **At the end of the story, Arlindo probably feels**

Ⓐ angry

Ⓑ happy

Ⓒ surprised

Ⓓ cheated

Why did you choose your answer?

_____

_____

_____

Good Test Takers

Think—Can I eliminate any answer choices?

4 **What detail from the story best shows the answer to Question 3?**

Ⓐ Arlindo was picked first for the practice game.

Ⓑ Arlindo was picked last for the practice game.

Ⓒ Arlindo learned there was no soccer team.

Ⓓ Arlindo's parents asked him about school.

Why did you choose your answer?

_____

_____

_____

DIRECTIONS: Read question 5 again and the answer that is given. Then write about how your answer was the same as this answer. Or write how it was different from this answer. You will need to look back at what you wrote on the "Think About the Question" pages.

Good Test Takers

Think—What facts and details support my answer?

5 **Why does Arlindo say his second day at school was "awesome"?**

Answer: *He played well and made friends, and he learned the word "awesome" from Adam.*

How is this answer the same as or different from your answer?

_____

_____

_____

Think When You Read

DIRECTIONS: Now you will learn about the Special Olympics. Read and think about what makes the Special Olympics so special. Then answer the questions about what you read.

Take Me to the Game

The Special Olympics

Since 1896, athletes from around the world have come together every few years to compete in the Olympics. You have probably heard about the Olympics or seen the Olympics on television. But, the Olympics are not the only important sports competitions held for athletes around the world. The Special Olympics offers another.

Good Readers

Think—What do I think this passage will be about?

Think When You Read

1 What do you already know about competitions held by the Special Olympics organization?

_____

_____

_____

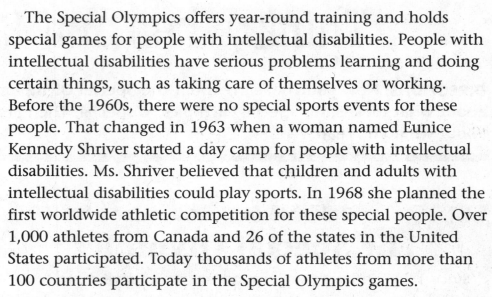

The Special Olympics offers year-round training and holds special games for people with intellectual disabilities. People with intellectual disabilities have serious problems learning and doing certain things, such as taking care of themselves or working. Before the 1960s, there were no special sports events for these people. That changed in 1963 when a woman named Eunice Kennedy Shriver started a day camp for people with intellectual disabilities. Ms. Shriver believed that children and adults with intellectual disabilities could play sports. In 1968 she planned the first worldwide athletic competition for these special people. Over 1,000 athletes from Canada and 26 of the states in the United States participated. Today thousands of athletes from more than 100 countries participate in the Special Olympics games.

The Special Olympics holds games in the summer and winter. In the summer games, athletes play Olympic-type sports like soccer, basketball, and tennis. They also do gymnastics and ride and jump horses. In the winter games, athletes play sports like figure skating and speed skating. They also snow ski and snowboard.

To take part in the games, athletes must be at least eight years old. Athletes must have some form of intellectual disability. These athletes get a lot from participating. The exercise makes them stronger. They become better able to do things with their bodies. They feel better about themselves and what they can do. Finally, they make friends from all over the world.

Think When You Read

2 Which of the Special Olympics sports would be the most interesting to see? Why do you think so?

_____

_____

_____

When Ms. Shriver planned the first games, she felt that all people with intellectual disabilities could receive these <u>benefits</u>. However, she did not think they had to be the fastest runner or best skier to do so. She believed that just by participating, people with intellectual disabilities could make their lives better and feel better about themselves. It is for this reason that all of the athletes in the games make this oath: "Let me win. But if I cannot win, let me be brave in the attempt."

©iStockphoto.com/Nikada33

Think When You Read

3 What do you think is the most important thing that people get from playing sports and games? Tell why you think so.

_____

_____

_____

Think About the Question

DIRECTIONS: Questions 1–5 have to do with the passage you just read. Write what you think the answer is to each question. Then tell why you wrote the answer that you wrote. You will answer these questions again on the "Think When You Answer" pages that follow.

Good Test Takers

Think—What does a *summarize* question ask?

1 **Which is the best summary of this story?**

Write a short summary of this story

_____

_____

What makes you think this is a possible answer?

_____

_____

Good Test Takers

Think—What does an *author's point of view* question ask?

2 **The person who wrote this story thinks the Special Olympics games are**

What do you think the answer to this question is?

_____

_____

What makes you think that?

_____

_____

3   **When did the Special Olympics competitions begin?**

What do you think the answer to this question is?

_____

_____

What makes you think that?

_____

_____

4   **In this story, the word <u>benefits</u> means**

What do you think the answer to this question is?

_____

_____

What makes you think that?

_____

_____

5   **Tell why winning is not the most important thing in the Special Olympics games.**

Explain what you think the answer is.

_____

_____

What makes you think that?

_____

_____

Think When You Answer

DIRECTIONS: Now look at questions 1–4 as they would appear on a test. Choose the **best** possible answer to each question. You may look back at what you wrote on the "Think About the Question" pages to help choose the correct answer.

Good Test Takers

Think—Can I eliminate any answer choices?

1. **Which is the best summary of this story?**

Ⓐ Special Olympics began in 1968.

Ⓑ Athletes play different sports in summer and winter.

Ⓒ Special Olympics gives special athletes a chance to learn.

Ⓓ Athletes in Special Olympics games become stronger.

> **Why did you choose your answer?**
>
> _____
>
> _____
>
> _____

2 The person who wrote this story thinks the Special Olympics games are

Ⓐ not as fun as the Olympics

Ⓑ as important as the Olympics

Ⓒ too much like the Olympics

Ⓓ held too often

Why did you choose your answer?

_____

_____

_____

3 When did the Special Olympics competitions begin?

Ⓐ 1896

Ⓑ 1960

Ⓒ 1963

Ⓓ 1968

Why did you choose your answer?

_____

_____

_____

Think—Can I eliminate any answer choices?

4 In this story, the word <u>benefits</u> means

Ⓐ things that help a person

Ⓑ prizes for winning

Ⓒ ways of getting money

Ⓓ problems with a person's mind

Why did you choose your answer?

_____

_____

DIRECTIONS: Read question 5 again and the answer that is given. Then write about how your answer was the same as this answer. Or write how it was different from this answer. You will need to look back at what you wrote on the "Think About the Question" pages.

Think—What facts and details support my answer?

5 Tell why winning is not the most important thing in the Special Olympics games.

Answer: *Athletes in the Special Olympics games learn a lot and make friends, too.*

How is this answer the same as or different from your answer?

_____

_____

_____

Theme Question

DIRECTIONS: The extended-response question below requires you to think about more than one of the passages you have just read. Read the question carefully and write your answer in the space provided. Use complete sentences, correct punctuation, and proper grammar. Be sure to answer each part of the question.

EXTENDED-RESPONSE QUESTION
THEME 2: TAKE ME TO THE GAME

What are some reasons why people enjoy playing sports? How are sports good for people? Explain what people can expect to get out of playing sports.

Use details from the passages you have just read to support your answer.

_____

_____

_____

_____

_____

_____

_____

_____

_____

_____

_____

_____

_____

Introduction to Theme 3:

What Makes Me, Me?

If someone asks you to tell about yourself, what do you tell? Do you tell about your looks, your family, where you live, or how you act? Many things make each of us special. We are each different in the way our bodies grow and look.

We are different in other ways, too. We live with different families and in different places. Our experiences make us different from others.

Each of us also acts differently. Some of us are friendly. Others are shy. Some of us are loud, while others are quiet. Why are we like we are? It might be because of information that is in our bodies, like information that tells us how tall we will grow. Or it might be because of our experiences. Scientists are still learning about what makes each of us who we are.

Now you will read three stories. These three stories tell about the different things that help to make you, you!

Think When You Read

1 What is something special about you?

_____

_____

_____

Think When You Read

DIRECTIONS: Now you will read about an activity that will help you think about why you are the way you are. Think about what you read. Then answer the questions.

Good Readers

Think—What do I think this passage will be about?

What Makes Me, Me?

Why Are You, You?

We are the same in many ways. And yet each of us is different, too. No one else is just like you.

Each of us is a mix of both of our parents. Our eye color, hair color, and nose shape are our physical traits. The ways we act, such as being shy, funny, or serious, are our personality traits. We get our physical traits from our parents. Our personalities can come from our parents and from our experiences with other people.

We can often see where we got our traits. For example, let's say your mother is left-handed and your father is right-handed. If you are left-handed, you probably got this physical trait from your mother.

This activity will help you think about where people get their traits.

What you'll need*:

Pencil

You and your parents or the adults with whom you spend a lot of time.

You can do this activity using a friend instead of yourself. Choose a friend whose parents you also know.

Think When You Read

1 How do you think you get traits from your parents and the other people you grow up around?

_____

_____

_____

What you'll do:

1. Fill in the table with your traits.

2. Fill in the table with the traits of your father.

3. Fill in the table with the traits of your mother.

4. Fill in the table with the traits of another adult with whom you spend a lot of time.

5. Compare the lists. This comparison will help you see where your traits come from!

Trait	Your or Your Friend's Trait	Father's Trait	Mother's Trait	Other Adult's Trait
Hair (dark or light)				
Eyes (color)				
Nose (turned up or turned down)				
Handedness (right or left)				
Quiet or talks a lot				
Serious or funny				

Think When You Read

2 Does this activity seem interesting to you? Tell why or why not.

_____

_____

_____

Think About the Question

DIRECTIONS: Questions 1–5 have to do with the passage you just read. Write what you think the answer is to each question. Then tell why you wrote the answer that you wrote. You will answer these questions again on the "Think When You Answer" pages that follow.

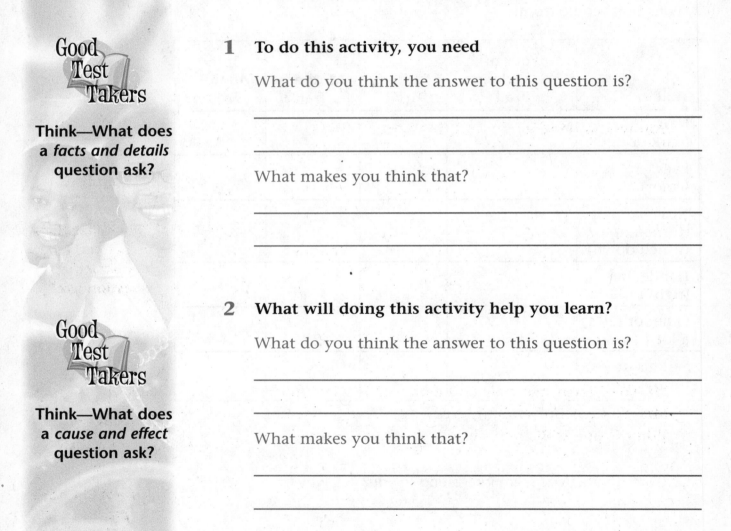

Good Test Takers

Think—What does a *facts and details* question ask?

1 **To do this activity, you need**

What do you think the answer to this question is?

_____

_____

What makes you think that?

_____

_____

Good Test Takers

Think—What does a *cause and effect* question ask?

2 **What will doing this activity help you learn?**

What do you think the answer to this question is?

_____

_____

What makes you think that?

_____

_____

3 **Which example does *not* show a physical trait that people get from their parents?**

Write a physical trait that a person would not get from his or her parents.

_____

_____

What makes you think this is a possible answer?

_____

_____

Think—What does an *inferences and conclusions* question ask?

4 **You would most likely find this activity in a book called**

Write a possible title of a book you would read.

_____

_____

What makes you think this is a possible answer?

_____

_____

Think—What does a *genres and types of passages* question ask?

5 **Mr. Fox has brown hair and eyes and is left-handed. Mrs. Fox has brown hair, green eyes, and is left-handed. What is one trait their child will likely have?**

What do you think the answer to this question is?

_____

_____

What makes you think that?

_____

_____

Think—What does a *prediction* question ask?

Think When You Answer

DIRECTIONS: Now look at questions 1–4 as they would appear on a test. Choose the **best** possible answer to each question. You may look back at what you wrote on the "Think About the Question" pages to help choose the correct answer.

Good Test Takers

Think—Can I eliminate any answer choices?

1 To do this activity, you need

Ⓐ two different people

Ⓑ any three people who look alike

Ⓒ a person and his or her parents

Ⓓ a person and his or her sister or brother

Why did you choose your answer?

_____

_____

_____

2 **What will doing this activity help you learn?**

Ⓐ why you are the way you are

Ⓑ why your parents look the way they do

Ⓒ where feelings come from

Ⓓ what traits are made of

Why did you choose your answer?

_____

_____

3 **Which example does *not* show a physical trait that people get from their parents?**

Ⓐ Juan is tall.

Ⓑ Sarah has short hair.

Ⓒ Jasmine has brown eyes.

Ⓓ Michael has big feet.

Why did you choose your answer?

_____

_____

Good Test Takers

Think—Can I eliminate any answer choices?

4 You would most likely find this activity in a book called

Ⓐ *Easy Ways to Teach Kids Math*

Ⓑ *Visiting People Around the World*

Ⓒ *Art Projects for a Rainy Day*

Ⓓ *Science Activities for Kids*

Why did you choose your answer?

_____

_____

_____

DIRECTIONS: Read question 5 again and the answer that is given. Then write about how your answer was the same as this answer. Or write how it was different from this answer. You will need to look back at what you wrote on the "Think About the Question" pages.

Good Test Takers

Think—What facts and details support my answer?

5 Mr. Fox has brown hair and eyes and is left-handed. Mrs. Fox has brown hair, green eyes, and is left-handed. What is one trait their child will likely have?

Answer: *Brown hair or left-handed*

How is this answer the same as or different from your answer?

_____

_____

_____

Think When You Read

DIRECTIONS: Here is a story about a girl who has grown up both Japanese and American. Read and think about the story. Then answer the questions about the story.

What Makes Me, Me?

Chopsticks and Forks

Sometimes when friends come to my house, they ask why I set the table with chopsticks* and also with a knife, fork, and spoon. This is the story that tells why.

My name is Emily. My mother is from Osaka, Japan. My father is from San Francisco, California. They met while they were students in California. My father was studying Japanese. My mother was teaching a Japanese conversation class to make money so she could study English.

When my father asked my mother to marry him, she said she would, but only on one condition. My father had to come to Japan to learn about my mother's culture. He said yes before she had finished the sentence.

Chopsticks are thin sticks that some Asian people use to eat with.

Good Readers

Think—What do I think this passage will be about?

Think When You Read

1 Why do you think Emily's father said yes so quickly?

_____

_____

_____

My mother and father lived in Japan for seven years after they were married. They taught English there. I was born there, but we moved to the United States when I was five. My mother and father were sad to leave Japan, but they had good jobs in the United States.

When we got back, my father said we should keep practicing Japanese customs. My mother insisted that I should grow up as an American.

For a long time, every time my mother left the house, my father taught me about Japan. When Dad made my lunch, he gave me chopsticks and Japanese foods, like vegetables and rice wrapped in seaweed. At night before bed, Dad sat in my room and told me stories about Japan. He told me how Japanese people take off their shoes and bow in the doorway before entering a house.

When Mom was home, though, we did everything the way she thought Americans should. She made peanut butter and jelly sandwiches for lunch even though she did not like them. She took me to movies so I would learn more about Americans. I told her those Americans did not seem as real as the Americans at my school, but she insisted that I would learn from the movies.

Think When You Read

2 Why do you think her father told her about Japan?

_____

_____

_____

One day I decided to put an end to this. My parents were forgetting that I am both Japanese and American. I didn't see why we couldn't live that way.

One afternoon when they were at work, I asked my babysitter to help me fix dinner. We made a huge meal. We made Japanese rice, fish, and vegetables. And, we made hamburgers. I set the table with chopsticks and with knives, forks, and spoons.

When my parents came home, I bowed to them. I asked them to take their shoes off at the front door. In the dining room, I had American rock-and-roll music playing. They looked at each other and laughed. "Emily, we get the message," they said.

"Finally," I said.

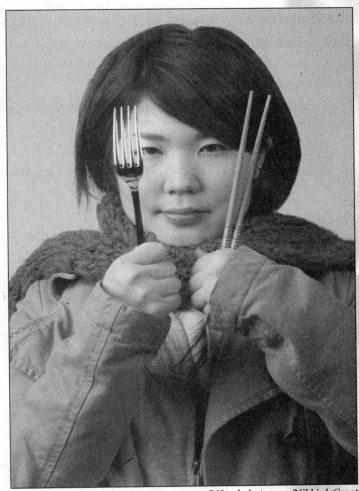

©iStockphoto.com/Nikki deGroot

Think When You Read

3 How do you think things were different for this family after this dinner?

_____

_____

_____

Think About the Question

DIRECTIONS: Questions 1–5 have to do with the passage you just read. Write what you think the answer is to each question. Then tell why you wrote the answer that you wrote. You will answer these questions again on the "Think When You Answer" pages that follow.

Good Test Takers

Think—What does a *text organization* question ask?

1 **The first paragraph of this story tells mostly about**

What do you think the answer to this question is?

_____

_____

What makes you think that?

_____

_____

Good Test Takers

Think—What does a *sequence* question ask?

2 **What happens first in this story?**

What do you think the answer to this question is?

_____

_____

What makes you think that?

_____

_____

3 **Why did Emily's parents move to Japan?**

What do you think the answer to this question is?

_____

_____

What makes you think that?

_____

_____

Good Test Takers

Think—What does a _cause and effect_ question ask?

4 **When she cooks dinner, Emily makes**

What do you think the answer to this question is?

_____

_____

What makes you think that?

_____

_____

Good Test Takers

Think—What does a _facts and details_ question ask?

5 **What is the message that Emily's parents get at the end of this story?**

What do you think the answer to this question is?

_____

_____

What makes you think that?

_____

_____

Good Test Takers

Think—What does an _inferences and conclusions_ question ask?

Think When You Answer

DIRECTIONS: Now look at questions 1–4 as they would appear on a test. Choose the **best** possible answer to each question. You may look back at what you wrote on the "Think About the Question" pages to help choose the correct answer.

Good Test Takers

Think—Can I eliminate any answer choices?

1 The first paragraph of this story tells mostly about
Ⓐ why this family eats with chopsticks
Ⓑ what question this story will answer
Ⓒ how Emily's parents met
Ⓓ where Emily's family lives

Why did you choose your answer?

_____

_____

_____

2 **What happens first in this story?**

(A) Emily's parents move to the United States.

(B) Emily's parents move to Japan.

(C) Emily's mother teaches Japanese.

(D) Emily is born.

Why did you choose your answer?

_____

_____

_____

3 **Why did Emily's parents move to Japan?**

(A) for her mother to learn to speak Japanese

(B) for her father to learn about Japanese culture

(C) for Emily to visit Japan

(D) to study in Japan

Why did you choose your answer?

_____

_____

_____

Good Test Takers

Think—Can I eliminate any answer choices?

4 When she cooks dinner, Emily makes

(A) Japanese and American food

(B) Mexican and Chinese food

(C) Japanese food only

(D) American food only

Why did you choose your answer?

_____

_____

_____

DIRECTIONS: Read question 5 again and the answer that is given. Then write about how your answer was the same as this answer. Or write how it was different from this answer. You will need to look back at what you wrote on the "Think About the Question" pages.

Good Test Takers

Think—What facts and details support my answer?

5 What is the message that Emily's parents get at the end of this story?

Answer: *Emily wants her family to live as Japanese and Americans.*

How is this answer the same as or different from your answer?

_____

_____

_____

Think When You Read

DIRECTIONS: Now you will read about the genes that work in your body to make you look and grow the way you do. Read and think about your genes. Then answer the questions.

What Makes Me, Me?

Look at My Genes!

Have you ever thought about what it would be like to have a trunk like an elephant or a neck like a giraffe? What about a fur coat like a dog or the hooves of a horse? Why do you look like you and not like an elephant, giraffe, dog, or horse? It is because all living things have genes that tell them what to be and how to grow.

Genes are tiny pieces of information. They are inside packages called chromosomes. Your chromosomes are inside of things called cells. All living things are made of cells. Some living things are made of only one cell. But other living things have many more cells than that. Think about your body, for example. It has about 100 trillion (100,000,000,000,000) cells.

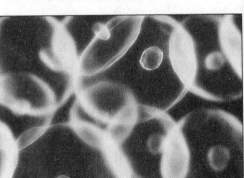

©iStockphoto.com/ERaxion

Good Readers

Think—What do I think this passage will be about?

Think When You Read

1 What is one thing that is the same in animals and plants? What is one thing that is different?

_____

_____

_____

Chromosomes are in each of your cells. They are in the cells of animals and plants, too. But the number of chromosomes is different. Every living thing has a certain number of chromosomes in each of its cells. For example, a mosquito has 6 chromosomes. A sunflower has 34. A cat has 38. A human has 46, and a dog has 78.

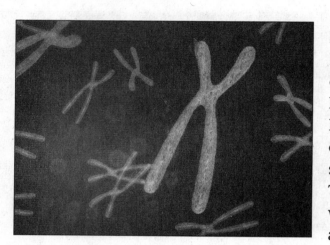

Each chromosome holds different genes. If you think of chromosomes like a long chain, a gene is like one link in the chain. Genes contain specific directions. Those directions tell what you look like and how you act.

Every gene does something different. For example, some genes determine the color of your eyes. Others determine the color of your hair. Thanks to genes, you have your nose and not an elephant's trunk. The genes you have tell about the parts of you that are different from other living things, including other people. Genes make you similar to other people, but they also make you one of a kind.

Think When You Read

2 What might happen if your genes got confused?

_____

_____

_____

Different living things have different numbers of genes. You have about 30,000 genes, and they are in each cell of your body. So each little part of your body has the same recipe book. But, although the same instructions are in each cell, not all of the genes work all of the time.

Genes are like switches. Inside each cell, some genes are turned off and some are turned on. That is a good thing because it means your nose doesn't grow where one of your ears should be.

Scientists are trying to learn how to switch genes on and off. They want to program genes to help us. For example, your body makes new skin cells for as long as you live. As you grow older, however, your body isn't able to make new cells as fast as it did when you were young. It takes longer for a cut to heal. If scientists could figure out how to turn on the genes that make new skin cells form, they could help people heal faster and have healthy skin even as they age.

The more we learn about genes, the more we learn about what makes you, you. Think about your genes! They make you special.

Think When You Read

3 What are some things that might happen if scientists learn how to turn genes on and off?

_____

_____

_____

Think About the Question

DIRECTIONS: Questions 1–5 have to do with the passage you just read. Write what you think the answer is to each question. Then tell why you wrote the answer that you wrote. You will answer these questions again on the "Think When You Answer" pages that follow.

Good Test Takers

Think—What does a *compare and contrast* question ask?

1 People's cells are a lot like cats' cells *except* that people have

What do you think the answer to this question is?

_____

_____

What makes you think that?

_____

_____

Good Test Takers

Think—What does a *compare and contrast* question ask?

2 Which is the biggest: a cell, a chromosome, or a gene?

What do you think the answer to this question is?

_____

_____

What makes you think that?

_____

_____

3 **In this story, the words <u>figure out</u> mean**

What do you think the answer to this question is?

_____

_____

What makes you think that?

_____

_____

Think—What does a *words and phrases* question ask?

4 **If you wanted to find more information like this, what kind of book would you look in?**

What do you think the answer to this question is?

_____

_____

What makes you think that?

_____

_____

Think—What does a *research and reference skills* question ask?

5 **What do genes do inside your body?**

What do you think the answer to this question is?

_____

_____

What makes you think that?

_____

_____

Think—What does a *summarize* question ask?

Think When You Answer

DIRECTIONS: Now look at questions 1–4 as they would appear on a test. Choose the **best** possible answer to each question. You may look back at what you wrote on the "Think About the Question" pages to help choose the correct answer.

Good Test Takers

Think—Can I eliminate any answer choices?

1 People's cells are a lot like cats' cells *except* that people have

Ⓐ more chromosomes

Ⓑ fewer chromosomes

Ⓒ no chromosomes

Ⓓ larger chromosomes

Why did you choose your answer?

_____

_____

_____

2 **Which is the biggest: a cell, a chromosome, or a gene?**

Ⓐ a cell

Ⓑ a chromosome

Ⓒ a gene

Ⓓ They are the same size.

Why did you choose your answer?

_____

_____

_____

3 **In this story, the words figure out mean**

Ⓐ forget

Ⓑ remember

Ⓒ learn

Ⓓ make

Why did you choose your answer?

_____

_____

_____

Think—Can I eliminate any answer choices?

4 If you wanted to find more information like this, what kind of book would you look in?

Ⓐ an atlas

Ⓑ a dictionary

Ⓒ a science book

Ⓓ a history book

Why did you choose your answer?

_____

_____

_____

DIRECTIONS: Read question 5 again and the answer that is given. Then write about how your answer was the same as this answer. Or write how it was different from this answer. You will need to look back at what you wrote on the "Think About the Question" pages.

Think—What facts and details support my answer?

5 What do genes do inside your body?

Answer: *They tell your body what to look like.*

How is this answer the same as or different from your answer?

_____

_____

_____

Theme Question

DIRECTIONS: The extended-response question below requires you to think about more than one of the passages you have just read. Read the question carefully and write your answer in the space provided. Use complete sentences, correct punctuation, and proper grammar. Be sure to answer each part of the question.

EXTENDED-RESPONSE QUESTION
THEME 3: WHAT MAKES ME, ME?

What determines how a person looks and acts? Why might a person look and act differently than one of his or her parents?

Use details from the passages you have just read to support your answer.

_____

_____

_____

_____

_____

_____

_____

_____

_____

_____

_____

_____

_____

_____

Introduction to Theme 4:

Flights of Discovery

People have long been interested in flying. This might be because it is a challenge to do something we cannot do without the help of a machine. This might also be because flying takes us to places we could not reach by car, bus, or train. It takes us across countries, mountains, and oceans. It even takes us into space.

Whatever the reason, our interest in flight has led to great discoveries. We can board an airplane and visit almost anywhere in the world. We can fly on spaceships to the moon. Someday, we might even fly to other planets.

Now you will read three stories. These stories each tell something about flight and space.

Think When You Read

1 What interests you about flying or space?

_____

_____

_____

Think When You Read

DIRECTIONS: Now you will learn about making paper airplanes. Think about what you read and then answer the questions.

Good Readers

Think—What do I think this passage will be about?

Flights of Discovery
How Does It Fly?

Making a paper airplane is a good way to learn about flying. Doing this activity with the students in your class will help you learn about flight.

What you'll need:

Paper and tape to make the airplane

One paper clip

One long piece of rope or tape

One blank piece of paper

What to do:

1. Make your paper airplane. You can fold paper in different ways to make an airplane. If you have not made an airplane before, try folding a sheet of paper in half. Then fold the outer sides down for wings. You can fold the wings so that the plane has a pointed front. Fold your paper in different ways to make different paper airplane shapes.

Think When You Read

1 Have you ever made a paper airplane? Tell about that time.

_____

_____

_____

2. Try a few test flights. See how far your airplane flies each time. Make lines on the ground with tape or rope to show how far each plane flies.

3. Put your paper clip on the front of your airplane. Fly your plane. How well does it fly now?

4. Put the paper clip on different parts of your plane. Where can you put the paper clip to help your plane fly the farthest?

5. Use your tape or rope to make big and small circles on the ground. Try to fly your airplane into the middle of each circle.

6. Compare your airplane with the airplanes your friends have made. Which kind of airplane flew the farthest? Which kind of airplane landed best inside the tape circles? Talk as a class about what you learned about flying.

©avesun/dreamstime.com

Think When You Read

2 What do you think you could learn from doing this activity?

_____

_____

_____

Think About the Question

DIRECTIONS: Questions 1–5 have to do with the passage you just read. Write what you think the answer is to each question. Then tell why you wrote the answer that you wrote. You will answer these questions again on the "Think When You Answer" pages that follow.

Good Test Takers

Think—What does an *author's* *point of view* question ask?

1 **The writer thinks that paper airplanes are**

What do you think the answer to this question is?

_____

_____

What makes you think that?

_____

_____

Good Test Takers

Think—What does a *facts and details* question ask?

2 **You need your paper clip for which steps?**

What do you think the answer to this question is?

_____

_____

What makes you think that?

_____

_____

3 **The circles of tape or rope are used to tell**

What do you think the answer to this question is?

_____

_____

What makes you think that?

_____

_____

Good Test Takers

Think—What does an *inferences and conclusions* question ask?

4 **This was written in order to**

What do you think the answer to this question is?

_____

_____

What makes you think that?

_____

_____

Good Test Takers

Think—What does an *author's purpose* question ask?

5 **Why is the last step, Step 6, important for learning about flying?**

What do you think the answer to this question is?

_____

_____

What makes you think that?

_____

_____

Good Test Takers

Think—What does an *inferences and conclusions* question ask?

Think When You Answer

DIRECTIONS: Now look at questions 1–4 as they would appear on a test. Choose the <u>best</u> possible answer to each question. You may look back at what you wrote on the "Think About the Question" pages to help choose the correct answer.

Good Test Takers

Think—Can I eliminate any answer choices?

1 **The writer thinks that paper airplanes are**

Ⓐ a way to keep children out of trouble

Ⓑ less interesting than real planes

Ⓒ more interesting than real planes

Ⓓ a good way to learn about flying

Why did you choose your answer?

_____

_____

_____

2 **You need your paper clip for which steps?**

Ⓐ 1 and 2

Ⓑ 2 and 3

Ⓒ 3 and 4

Ⓓ 4 and 5

Why did you choose your answer?

_____

_____

_____

3 **The circles of tape or rope are used to tell**

Ⓐ which airplanes go where you want them to

Ⓑ which airplane is the most difficult to make

Ⓒ how far each airplane can fly

Ⓓ how large each airplane is

Why did you choose your answer?

_____

_____

_____

Good Test Takers

Think—Can I eliminate any answer choices?

4 **This was written in order to**

Ⓐ tell about real airplanes

Ⓑ teach how things fly

Ⓒ show how to make different paper toys

Ⓓ list ways to use paper clips on planes

Why did you choose your answer?

_____

_____

_____

DIRECTIONS: Read question 5 again and the answer that is given. Then write about how your answer was the same as this answer. Or write how it was different from this answer. You will need to look back at what you wrote on the "Think About the Question" pages.

Good Test Takers

Think—What facts and details support my answer?

5 **Why is the last step, Step 6, important for learning about flying?**

Answer: *You can find out which kind of plane flies the best.*

How is this answer the same as or different from your answer?

_____

_____

_____

Think When You Read

DIRECTIONS: This story takes place in the year 2075 after Joneka has gone to live on Planet Synon. Read to find out what happens to her there. Then answer the questions about the story.

Flights of Discovery
Not So Different After All

Good Readers

It was the year 2075. Joneka sat awake in her sleeping chair, watching the sky turn a brilliant green. She had lived on Planet Synon for one month and still wasn't used to the sky's color. She missed the shades of blue in Earth's sky.

Think—What do I think this passage will be about?

©iStockphoto.com/Michael Knight

She had not adjusted to anything about Synon. There were just a few houses on her street, and there were no Earth children her age. Joneka and her mother had been chosen to go to Synon because Joneka's mother was a scientist. Joneka's mother was there to study the Syns, the people who lived on Synon.

Joneka thought of the crowded street where she had lived on Earth. She thought of her dome, with its schools, stores, and special outdoor zones that had trees and plants. The dome was so big that she did not know all of the people who lived there, but she had lots of friends. On Synon, there were not even enough people to make a dome.

Think When You Read

1 How is where Joneka lives different from where you live?

_____

_____

_____

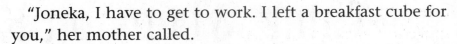

"Joneka, I have to get to work. I left a breakfast cube for you," her mother called.

Joneka got up, grabbed her breakfast cube, and walked outside. She knew she should stay close to home. She was not supposed to get close to any of the Syns because her parents warned that Syns were different and unkind. But Joneka was tired of staying close to home. When she saw that no one was watching, she walked to the end of her street and kept going.

Joneka walked for a long time over an uneven path that was covered with blue rocks. She was so lost in her thoughts that she did not even notice the Syn. "Why sad?" he asked.

Joneka was so surprised that she stumbled and fell over one of the rocks. A shot of pain rose from her ankle when she tried to stand. She saw the Syn running away. She thought he had seemed friendly, but now she wondered if her parents were right about the Syns.

"I doubt he is going to get help," Joneka thought. She wished she had never left her house. She called her mother with her watch phone, but her mom was not there. Joneka left a message, telling her mom where she was.

Think When You Read

2 What do you think is going to happen next?

_____

_____

_____

Just then, the Syn came back. He had another Syn with him, who spoke to Joneka. "Pertrux brought me because I speak English. My name is Rador. Pertrux will fix your ankle." While Pertrux wrapped her ankle, Rador asked her questions about Earth. He was very curious. He had learned to speak English from watching the Earth television he had made in science class. Science was Rador's favorite class, just like it was for Joneka.

©iStockphoto.com/Kian Eriksen

Just as Pertrux finished wrapping her ankle, Joneka's mother sped up in her electric car. "Don't touch my daughter!" she screamed when she saw Pertrux kneeling near Joneka.

"Mom," said Joneka, "Calm down. He was helping me, not hurting me. And it turns out we were wrong about the Syns. They are not so different after all."

Think When You Read

3 How do you think Joneka's life on Synon is going to change after this?

_____

_____

_____

Think About the Question

DIRECTIONS: Questions 1–5 have to do with the passage you just read. Write what you think the answer is to each question. Then tell why you wrote the answer that you wrote. You will answer these questions again on the "Think When You Answer" pages that follow.

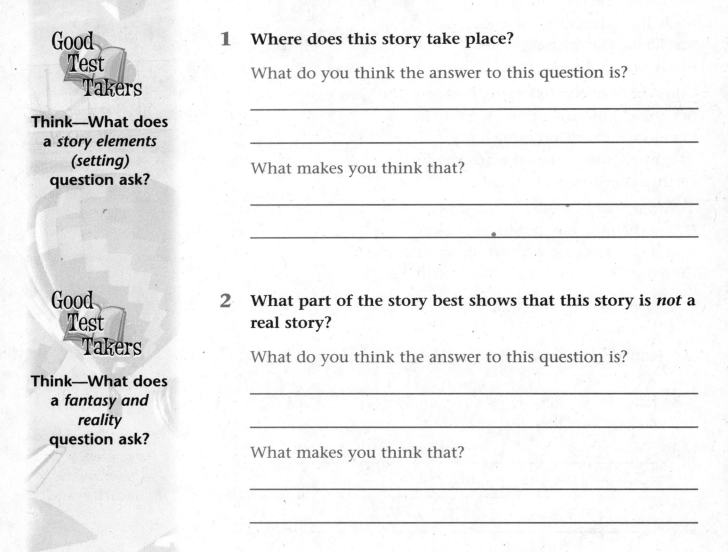

Good Test Takers

Think—What does a *story elements* (setting) question ask?

1 **Where does this story take place?**

What do you think the answer to this question is?

_____

_____

What makes you think that?

_____

_____

Good Test Takers

Think—What does a *fantasy and reality* question ask?

2 **What part of the story best shows that this story is *not* a real story?**

What do you think the answer to this question is?

_____

_____

What makes you think that?

_____

_____

3 **How does Joneka feel at the beginning of this story?**

What do you think the answer to this question is?

_____

_____

What makes you think that?

_____

_____

Good Test Takers

Think—What does an *inferences and conclusions* question ask?

4 **Which of the following best tells the theme of this story?**

Write a sentence that explains the theme of this story.

_____

_____

What makes you think this is a possible answer?

_____

_____

Good Test Takers

Think—What does a *story elements (theme)* question ask?

5 **How do Joneka's feelings about Synon change in the story?**

What do you think the answer to this question is?

_____

_____

What makes you think that?

_____

_____

Good Test Takers

Think—What does an *inferences and conclusions* question ask?

Think When You Answer

DIRECTIONS: Now look at questions 1–4 as they would appear on a test. Choose the **best** possible answer to each question. You may look back at what you wrote on the "Think About the Question" pages to help choose the correct answer.

Good Test Takers

Think—Can I eliminate any answer choices?

1 **Where does this story take place?**

Ⓐ in a dream Joneka has

Ⓑ on the planet Earth

Ⓒ on a spaceship

Ⓓ on the planet Synon

> **Why did you choose your answer?**
>
> _____
>
> _____
>
> _____

2 **What part of the story best shows that this story is *not* a real story?**

Ⓐ Joneka watched the sky turn a brilliant green.

Ⓑ Joneka fell over a rock.

Ⓒ Joneka wished she had never left her house.

Ⓓ Science was Rador and Joneka's favorite class.

Why did you choose your answer?

_____

_____

_____

3 **How does Joneka feel at the beginning of this story?**

Ⓐ excited

Ⓑ lonely

Ⓒ proud

Ⓓ scared

Why did you choose your answer?

_____

_____

_____

Good Test Takers

Think—Can I eliminate any answer choices?

4 **Which of the following best tells the theme of this story?**

Ⓐ It is best to follow the rules.

Ⓑ People who seem different may be more like you than you think.

Ⓒ A twisted ankle can lead to serious problems.

Ⓓ Wherever you go, do not forget where you came from.

Why did you choose your answer?

_____

_____

_____

DIRECTIONS: Read question 5 again and the answer that is given. Then write about how your answer was the same as this answer. Or write how it was different from this answer. You will need to look back at what you wrote on the "Think About the Question" pages.

Good Test Takers

Think—What facts and details support my answer?

5 **How do Joneka's feelings about Synon change in the story?**

Answer: *She was lonely at first, but in the end, she makes friends with some Syns and starts to feel better.*

How is this answer the same as or different from your answer?

_____

_____

_____

106

Think When You Read

DIRECTIONS: Now you will learn about Ellen Ochoa, the first Hispanic-American woman to become an astronaut. Read and think about what you read. Then answer the questions.

Flights of Discovery

Ellen Ochoa: Astronaut

Imagine flying high in outer space and looking down at the earth below. Earth would look like a spinning ball with large, bright blue spots. Ellen Ochoa has seen Earth from far, far away during the several trips she has taken on board space shuttles. Ellen Ochoa is an astronaut. She flies into space to study Earth and the space around it.

Courtesy NASA

Good Readers

Think—What do I think this passage will be about?

Think When You Read

1 Would you like to be an astronaut? Why or why not?

_____

_____

_____

Courtesy NASA

When she became an astronaut in 1991, Ellen Ochoa was the first Hispanic-American woman to do so. She had not always wanted to be an astronaut. Partly, this was because when she was a child, there were no women astronauts. So, she thought that being an astronaut was something that men did. It was not until after she finished college and was studying and doing research at Stanford University that Ellen Ochoa decided she wanted to be an astronaut.

Since becoming an astronaut, Ellen Ochoa has had several chances to go into space. There, she has studied how activity on the sun affects Earth. For Ellen Ochoa, going into space has always been exciting and never scary. She says that the training to go into space is always harder than the actual trip into space. This is because in training, astronauts learn what to do in case things go wrong. But space flights are carefully planned, and nothing has gone wrong during Ochoa's flights in space.

Think When You Read

2 Does going out into space sound exciting or scary to you? Tell why you think so.

_____

_____

_____

Although everything usually goes right, life in space is different. There is no gravity in space. Gravity is the force that pulls people and things towards Earth. Gravity is why we walk on the floor and not on the ceiling. In space, the astronauts float around inside their space shuttle. When they want to go to sleep, they find a place to hook their sleeping bags and then float as they sleep.

Ellen Ochoa has done amazing things in her job as an astronaut. But one of her favorite things is talking to students about her experiences. She likes to tell them about what she has done. That's because she wants to encourage students to study and work hard so that they have the chance to do interesting things with their lives, too.

Ellen Ochoa worked and studied her whole life, and her hard work has paid off. Now Ellen Ochoa is an astronaut who studies space up close.

Think When You Read

3 Why do you think Ellen Ochoa likes to talk to students about what she has done?

_____

_____

_____

Courtesy NASA

Think About the Question

DIRECTIONS: Questions 1–5 have to do with the passage you just read. Write what you think the answer is to each question. Then tell why you wrote the answer that you wrote. You will answer these questions again on the "Think When You Answer" pages that follow.

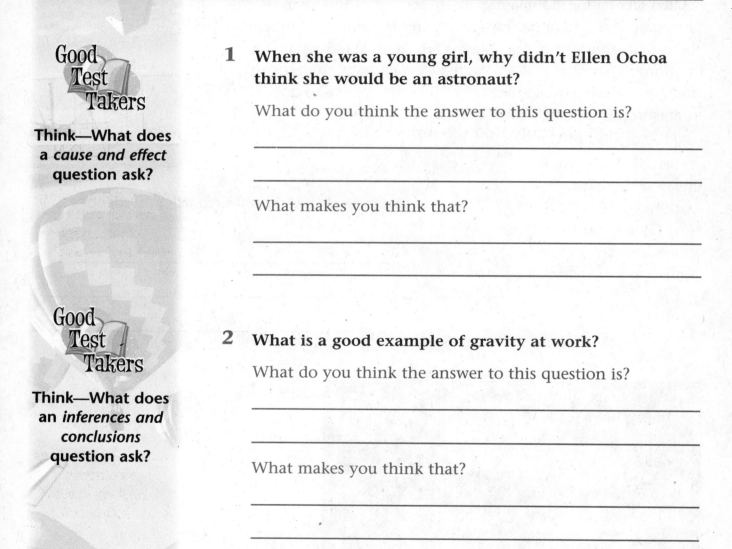

Good Test Takers

Think—What does a *cause and effect* question ask?

1 When she was a young girl, why didn't Ellen Ochoa think she would be an astronaut?

What do you think the answer to this question is?

_____

_____

What makes you think that?

_____

_____

Good Test Takers

Think—What does an *inferences and conclusions* question ask?

2 What is a good example of gravity at work?

What do you think the answer to this question is?

_____

_____

What makes you think that?

_____

_____

110

3 **What lesson could you learn from this story about Ellen Ochoa?**

What do you think the answer to this question is?

_____

_____

What makes you think that?

_____

_____

4 **You would probably find this story in a book called**

Write a possible title of a book you would read.

_____

_____

What makes you think this is a possible answer?

_____

_____

5 **Why does Ellen Ochoa say that training is harder than being in space?**

What do you think the answer to this question is?

_____

_____

What makes you think that?

_____

_____

Good Test Takers

Think—What does an *author's purpose* question ask?

Good Test Takers

Think—What does a *genres and types of passages* question ask?

Good Test Takers

Think—What does a *compare and contrast* question ask?

Think When You Answer

DIRECTIONS: Now look at questions 1–4 as they would appear on a test. Choose the **best** possible answer to each question. You may look back at what you wrote on the "Think About the Question" pages to help choose the correct answer.

Good Test Takers

Think—Can I
eliminate any
answer choices?

1 When she was a young girl, why didn't Ellen Ochoa think she would be an astronaut?

Ⓐ She did not like science.

Ⓑ She was not interested in space.

Ⓒ There were no women astronauts.

Ⓓ There had not been any trips to space.

Why did you choose your answer?

_____

_____

_____

2 **What is a good example of gravity at work?**

Ⓐ When you let go of something, it falls to the floor.

Ⓑ If you practice, you can become a faster runner.

Ⓒ People need to rest every day.

Ⓓ The sun shines in the day; the moon shines at night.

Why did you choose your answer?

_____

_____

_____

3 **What lesson could you learn from this story about Ellen Ochoa?**

Ⓐ Don't be afraid to follow the dreams you had as a child.

Ⓑ Be nice to other people if you want them to be nice to you.

Ⓒ It is not always the fastest person who wins the race.

Ⓓ If you work hard, you can be anything you want to be.

Why did you choose your answer?

_____

_____

_____

Good Test Takers

Think—Can I eliminate any answer choices?

4 **You would probably find this story in a book called**

Ⓐ *The Earth*

Ⓑ *The First Flight*

Ⓒ *Women in Space*

Ⓓ *Flying Machines*

Why did you choose your answer?

_____

_____

_____

DIRECTIONS: Read question 5 again and the answer that is given. Then write about how your answer was the same as this answer. Or write how it was different from this answer. You will need to look back at what you wrote on the "Think About the Question" pages.

Good Test Takers

Think—What facts and details support my answer?

5 **Why does Ellen Ochoa say that training is harder than being in space?**

Answer: *When they train, astronauts practice as if everything will go wrong. But in space, things usually go right.*

How is this answer the same as or different from your answer?

_____

_____

_____

Theme Question

DIRECTIONS: The extended-response question below requires you to think about more than one of the passages you have just read. Read the question carefully and write your answer in the space provided. Use complete sentences, correct punctuation, and proper grammar. Be sure to answer each part of the question.

EXTENDED-RESPONSE QUESTION

THEME 4: FLIGHTS OF DISCOVERY

What are some reasons why people want to fly? How does being able to fly help people?

Use details from the passages you have just read to support your answer.

_____

_____

_____

_____

_____

_____

_____

_____

_____

_____

_____

_____

Independent Practice
On Your Own

Theme 5: Holidays and Celebrations

Theme 6: Ancient Animals

Theme 7: Learning from Each Other

Using the Think Reading Strategy on Your Own

Now you will read stories and answer questions like those on reading tests. This section will allow you to practice using the *Think Reading* Strategy for Test Taking. Practicing will help you do your best when you take a test.

These stories do not have boxes with questions in them. However, you should still think while you read.

As you read, think about . . .
• what the stories are mostly about,
• what the stories remind you of, and
• what might happen next in the story.

Also think about . . .
• how the stories are the same as or different from other stories you have read, and
• how things that happen in these stories are like things that have happened to you.

Then, answer the questions. Most of the questions have answer choices with them. Follow these steps to choose the best answer for each question:

1. Before you look at the answer choices, make sure you know what each question is asking.

2. Think of your own answer for the question.

3. Choose an answer from the choices.

Introduction to Theme 5:

Holidays and Celebrations

Every culture has its own special holidays and celebrations. There are many important traditions associated with these special occassions. Read about some of them.

DIRECTIONS: Now you will read three stories about different holidays or celebrations. Read and think about each story. Then answer the questions.

Good Readers ask themselves questions about what they are reading and take notes:

_____

_____

_____

_____

_____

_____

_____

_____

_____

_____

Holidays and Celebrations
Potato Latkes

The word *latkes* sounds like "lot-keys." People eat these traditional fried potato pancakes on the Jewish holiday of Chanukah, the Festival of Lights. The pancakes are fried with oil. The oil is important because of something that happened on the first Chanukah long ago. A small amount of oil, only enough to burn in a lamp for one day, burned for eight days.

Today, Chanukah is celebrated in late November or early December. Chanukah lasts for eight days, and each day families light a candle or small oil lamp.

When you make latkes for Chanukah, be sure to make extras! They will be eaten quickly.

What you need:

2 potatoes	1/4 cup flour
1 egg (stirred)	vegetable oil (for frying)

What to do:

1. Peel and grate the potatoes.

2. Mix the potatoes with the egg and flour.

3. Heat the oil in a pan. You will need help with this.

4. Drop small spoonfuls of the mixture onto the pan.

5. Cook the latkes until they turn light brown on both sides.

6. Remove the latkes from the pan and put them onto a plate covered with a paper towel. The paper towel will soak up some of the oil that stays on the latkes.

©Lisafx/dreamstime.com

DIRECTIONS: Read each question carefully. Darken the circle for each correct answer. For Question 5, write your answer in the space below the question.

1 **In this recipe, the word <u>traditional</u> means**

Ⓐ healthful

Ⓑ new

Ⓒ not often done or made

Ⓓ usually done or made

> **Why did you choose your answer?**
>
> _____
>
> _____
>
> _____

2 **To find out more about Chanukah, you should**

Ⓐ read a cookbook

Ⓑ read a book about holidays

Ⓒ learn more about cooking

Ⓓ look up "latke" in the dictionary

> **Why did you choose your answer?**
>
> _____
>
> _____
>
> _____

3 **What is something you need to make latkes?**

Ⓐ a paper towel

Ⓑ brown sugar

Ⓒ a large oven

Ⓓ a cup of water

Why did you choose your answer?

_____

_____

4 **How does the writer try to interest you in making latkes?**

Ⓐ by telling that Chanukah lasts for eight days

Ⓑ by explaining how to say the word latke

Ⓒ by suggesting that you should make extras

Ⓓ by describing why the oil is important

Why did you choose your answer?

_____

_____

5 **What would happen if you did not follow Step 6?**

_____

_____

_____

_____

_____

_____

Why do you think this is the answer?

_____

_____

_____

Good Readers ask themselves questions about what they are reading and take notes:

_____

_____

_____

_____

_____

_____

_____

_____

_____

_____

_____

_____

_____

Holidays and Celebrations

The Kwanzaa Party That Almost Wasn't

Jalen woke before sunrise. At first, he was excited. It was Imani, the final day of Kwanzaa. For Jalen's family, this night was a special holiday. But then he remembered that his parents had gone to the hospital the night before because his mother was having a baby. They'd left Jalen with his grandmother. The house was quiet.

Jalen tiptoed to the room where his grandmother was sleeping. "Are you awake?" he whispered.

"Oh, dear," Granny replied, "I'm sick. I need to sleep."

Jalen didn't know what to do, but he knew this was not how Kwanzaa should be! He wanted his new brother or sister to return to a Kwanzaa celebration.

It was afternoon when Granny came into the kitchen.

"I feel better, and I think it is because of the marvelous smells coming from this kitchen! What are you doing?"

Jalen grinned. He pointed to the macaroni and cheese on the counter and the sweet potato pie cooling on the windowsill. "I've been cooking," he said. "I copied what I've seen you and Mama do, but I'm glad you're here."

©iStockphoto.com/Jack Puccio

Jalen and his grandmother were setting the table when his parents arrived.

©iStockphoto.com/Karcich

"The doctor said we could come home so Kiara could meet her big brother," his mother announced.

"You didn't have to cook, Mom," said Jalen's dad.

"It wasn't me," said Granny, pointing to Jalen.

"You have a lot to teach your baby sister!" said his mother.

"I'm ready," said Jalen, smiling.

Good Readers take notes:

_____

_____

_____

_____

_____

_____

DIRECTIONS: Read each question carefully. Darken the circle for each correct answer. For Question 5, write your answer in the space below the question.

1   **Why does Jalen wake up before sunrise?**

Ⓐ He woke early to cook dinner.

Ⓑ He was excited about Kwanzaa.

Ⓒ He had to go to the hospital.

Ⓓ He had to help his grandmother.

Why did you choose your answer?

_____

_____

_____

2 **How did Jalen learn to cook?**

Ⓐ He studied cooking at school.

Ⓑ He read about cooking in a book.

Ⓒ He watched his mother and grandmother.

Ⓓ He saw a show about cooking on television.

Why did you choose your answer?

_____

_____

_____

3 **How does Jalen feel at the end of this story?**

Ⓐ disappointed

Ⓑ uninterested

Ⓒ quiet

Ⓓ proud

Why did you choose your answer?

_____

_____

_____

4 **Which sentence from the story supports your answer to Question 3?**

Ⓐ Jalen woke before sunrise.

Ⓑ They'd left Jalen with his grandmother.

Ⓒ "You didn't have to cook, Mom," said Jalen's dad.

Ⓓ "I'm ready," said Jalen, smiling.

Why did you choose your answer?

_____

_____

_____

5 **Why does Jalen cook the Kwanzaa dinner for his family?**

_____

_____

_____

_____

_____

Why do you think this is the answer?

_____

_____

Good Readers ask themselves questions about what they are reading and take notes:

_____

_____

_____

_____

_____

_____

_____

_____

_____

_____

_____

Holidays and Celebrations
Día de los Muertos

People have different ways to remember their ancestors and loved ones who have died. Many cultures have special days to honor the dead. You might think these celebrations would be sad times. But in Mexico, the Day of the Dead, or Día de los Muertos, is a joyful celebration that happens every year at the beginning of November.

Instead of being sad, Mexicans take the Day of the Dead as a time to remember the happy times people had in life. Families go to cemeteries and clean around the graves of their loved ones. They leave flowers. They also prepare a large feast of Mexican foods. This is because many Mexicans believe that on this day, the souls of the dead come back to Earth to eat their favorite foods once again with the people they love.

There may be many reasons why Mexicans have celebrated the Day of the Dead in the fall for hundreds of years. The first reason might be that fall is a time when trees lose their leaves and Earth prepares for winter. Life slows down or stops. Another reason might be the butterflies. Thousands of butterflies come to Mexico in the fall. They are flying south where it will be warmer. Hundreds of years ago, people who lived in Mexico believed that these butterflies were the spirits of people who had died. This belief might also explain why the Day of the Dead is a joyful celebration.

©iStockphoto.com/CathyKeifer

Today, Mexicans across Mexico and the United States celebrate the Day of the Dead. For many, this is a special way to stay close to those who are living and those who are gone.

DIRECTIONS: Read each question carefully. Darken the circle for each correct answer. For Question 5, write your answer in the space below the question.

1 This story is mostly about

Ⓐ the history of Mexico

Ⓑ a special day for Mexicans

Ⓒ the seasons of the year

Ⓓ how to cook Mexican food

Why did you choose your answer?

_____

_____

2 In this story, the word <u>feast</u> means a

Ⓐ special meal

Ⓑ time of year

Ⓒ happy holiday

Ⓓ bunch of flowers

Why did you choose your answer?

_____

_____

3 The third paragraph is mostly about

Ⓐ what people do on the Day of the Dead

Ⓑ how to have a Day of the Dead celebration

Ⓒ who celebrates the Day of the Dead

Ⓓ why the Day of the Dead is in November

Why did you choose your answer?

_____

_____

_____

4 Which word best describes the Day of the Dead?

Ⓐ scary

Ⓑ sad

Ⓒ happy

Ⓓ boring

Why did you choose your answer?

_____

_____

_____

5 **Why do Mexicans celebrate the Day of the Dead?**

_____

_____

_____

_____

_____

Why do you think this is the answer?

_____

_____

_____

Theme Question

DIRECTIONS: The extended-response question below requires you to think about more than one of the passages you have just read. Read the question carefully and write your answer in the space provided. Use complete sentences, correct punctuation, and proper grammar. Be sure to answer each part of the question.

EXTENDED-RESPONSE QUESTION

THEME 5: HOLIDAYS AND CELEBRATIONS

Compare any two of the celebrations mentioned in the passages you just read. How are they alike? How are they different?

Use details from the passages you have just read to support your answer.

_____

_____

_____

_____

_____

_____

_____

_____

_____

_____

_____

_____

_____

Introduction to Theme 6:

Ancient Animals

Millions of years ago, giant animals walked on Earth. Some of these animals may look familiar and others not so familiar. Although these animals lived long ago, there are still ways in which we can learn more about them.

DIRECTIONS: Read these three stories about animals from long ago. Read and think about each story and answer the questions.

Good Readers

Good Readers ask themselves questions about what they are reading and take notes:

_____

_____

_____

_____

_____

_____

_____

_____

_____

_____

Ancient Animals

Map of the Ancient Animals Collection

Welcome to the third floor of the City Science Museum. Here you will find the Ancient Animals Collection! We hope this map will help you find your way as you discover animals that lived on Earth millions of years ago.

Here on the third floor, you can see pictures and bones of animals that lived long ago. In the first three rooms, you can see the dinosaurs. These were the largest animals to ever walk on Earth. The last dinosaurs lived during the Cretaceous Period, between 136 million years ago and 65 million years ago. At the end of this period, all the dinosaurs

©iStockphoto.com/woodstock

died. Life on Earth continued to change. In the last Ice Age, which ended about 10,000 years ago, large mammals lived. They included huge lions, rhinos, and elephant-like animals. To see the bones of all of the museum's ancient animals, be sure to walk through all of the rooms on the third floor!

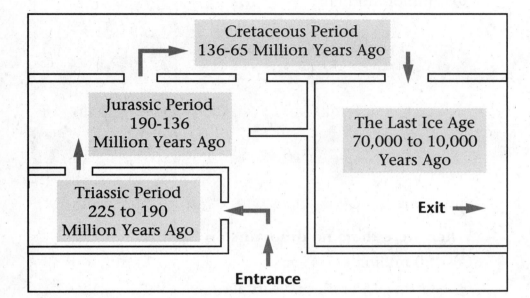

Good Readers take notes:

DIRECTIONS: Read each question carefully. Darken the circle for each correct answer. For Question 5, write your answer in the space below the question.

1 **This map helps people to**
Ⓐ learn more about different kinds of dinosaurs
Ⓑ learn about the third floor of the City Science Museum
Ⓒ know when they can visit the City Science Museum
Ⓓ know how to get to the City Science Museum

Why did you choose your answer?

2 **In the map, the word <u>Period</u> means a**

Ⓐ large amount of time

Ⓑ very short amount of time

Ⓒ way to end a sentence

Ⓓ kind of dinosaur

Why did you choose your answer?

_____

_____

_____

3 **When were there no dinosaurs on Earth?**

Ⓐ 190 million years ago

Ⓑ starting 150 million years ago

Ⓒ 136 million years ago

Ⓓ since 65 million years ago

Why did you choose your answer?

_____

_____

_____

4 **If you follow the arrows on the third floor, you will**

Ⓐ learn more about animals on Earth today

Ⓑ end up in the room that shows the Triassic Period

Ⓒ see animals in order of the time they lived on Earth

Ⓓ get to see small animals before you see large ones

Why did you choose your answer?

_____

_____

_____

5 **What is different about the last room from the first three rooms?**

_____

_____

_____

_____

_____

Why do you think this is the answer?

_____

_____

_____

Good Readers

Good Readers ask themselves questions about what they are reading and take notes:

_____
_____
_____
_____
_____
_____
_____
_____
_____
_____
_____
_____
_____
_____
_____

Ancient Animals
Backyard Bones

Joshua liked to dig. He knew the earth was old and wanted to see what he could find. He was trying to convince his friend, Matthew, to dig, too. Joshua told Matthew how he had once found an old Native-American arrowhead.

"I've only seen you find dirt," Matthew replied.

"Just wait. I might find something cool in your backyard," said Joshua.

"Go ahead. I'm going inside," said Matthew. "Find me when you get bored."

Matthew was wondering how soon Joshua was going to get bored when Joshua ran in with a wild look on his face. "You've got to come outside!" he said. "You won't believe what I've found."

When Matthew went outside, he saw that Joshua had dug a big hole in the corner of his yard. In the hole was a bone, a big bone. Joshua had only uncovered one end. When Matthew

©iStockphoto.com/Escaflowne

Good Readers take notes:

realized how big it was, he helped Joshua dig. By the end of the day, they could see the whole bone.

When they showed their parents the bone, Joshua's dad called the local college. The next day, a scientist who studies bones from ancient times came to Matthew's house. She took the bone to her research lab. At the end of the week, she asked the two boys to come to her lab.

"Well, boys," said the scientist, "you've found a bone from a mastodon, an animal that lived about 10,000 years ago. Do you think your parents will let us come dig for more bones in your yard?"

"I know they will," said Matthew. "Need any help digging?" he asked.

DIRECTIONS: Read each question carefully. Darken the circle for each correct answer. For Question 5, write your answer in the space below the question.

1 **About how old is the bone that the boys found?**
- Ⓐ 10 years old
- Ⓑ 100 years old
- Ⓒ 1,000 years old
- Ⓓ 10,000 years old

Why did you choose your answer?

_____

_____

_____

2 Why does Matthew help Joshua dig?

Ⓐ He likes digging.

Ⓑ He is bored.

Ⓒ He sees the big bone.

Ⓓ He wants to find an arrowhead.

Why did you choose your answer?

_____

_____

3 Where does most of this story take place?

Ⓐ in a science lab

Ⓑ in Joshua's backyard

Ⓒ in Matthew's backyard

Ⓓ in a zoo

Why did you choose your answer?

_____

_____

140

4 **What will probably happen next to Joshua and Matthew?**

Ⓐ They will decide that they are bored with digging.

Ⓑ They will help dig to find more bones.

Ⓒ They will get into trouble for digging in their yards.

Ⓓ They will decide to keep what they found a secret.

Why did you choose your answer?

_____

_____

_____

5 **How does Matthew feel about digging at the end of this story?**

_____

_____

_____

_____

_____

Why do you think this is the answer?

_____

_____

_____

Good Readers

Good Readers ask themselves questions about what they are reading and take notes:

_____

_____

_____

_____

_____

_____

_____

_____

_____

_____

_____

_____

_____

_____

_____

Ancient Animals

The La Brea Tar Pits

Walk around a busy American city today and try to picture what life was like on Earth thousands of years ago. It may be hard to do unless you visit Hancock Park in Los Angeles, California. Hancock Park is the home of the La Brea Tar Pits. People have found millions of bones of Ice Age animals within these pits.

The story of the La Brea Tar Pits began millions of years ago. Where Hancock Park is now, there was once oil deep under the ground. It seeped up through the earth, forming large puddles of tar on the ground. Above the ground, there were ponds and streams. When animals came to the water to drink, they got stuck in the tar. Many could not escape and died. Other animals came to eat these animals. These unlucky hunters often ended up stuck themselves. Their bones stayed in the tar, buried there for as long as 38,000 years.

In the early 1900s, scientists began digging in the area. They found the bones of ancient horses, mammoths, lions, saber-toothed tigers, and other animals. By looking at the bones and the soil around them, these scientists learned when these animals lived.

Scientists also found the bones of one person, a woman they called La Brea Woman. Her bones are 9,000 years old and are the oldest human bones that have ever been found in this part of California. Scientists have studied her bones to try to learn more about what life might have been like for a person living 9,000 years ago.

The La Brea Tar Pits are now a museum. People from all over the world come to see what this part of Los Angeles looked like thousands of years ago.

©Adambooth/dreamstime.com

DIRECTIONS: Read each question carefully. Darken the circle for each correct answer. For Question 5, write your answer in the space below the question.

1 Another good name for this story would be

Ⓐ "Stuck in Time"

Ⓑ "Looking for Clues"

Ⓒ "Los Angeles Today"

Ⓓ "Parks Around the World"

Why did you choose your answer?

_____

_____

2 Why did animals come to the area around the La Brea Tar Pits?

Ⓐ They liked to eat tar and oil.

Ⓑ They wanted water and food.

Ⓒ Water covered the rest of Los Angeles.

Ⓓ There was no other water to drink.

Why did you choose your answer?

_____

_____

3 **What is tar like?**

Ⓐ rocks

Ⓑ water

Ⓒ glue

Ⓓ dirt

Why did you choose your answer?

_____

_____

_____

4 **What have scientists learned from the bones in the La Brea Tar Pits?**

Ⓐ how plants and trees grow

Ⓑ why tar and oil are sticky

Ⓒ when different animals lived in that area

Ⓓ where the first animals and people came from

Why did you choose your answer?

_____

_____

_____

5 **Why are there so many bones in the La Brea Tar Pits?**

_____

_____

_____

_____

_____

Why do you think this is the answer?

_____

_____

_____

Theme Question

DIRECTIONS: The extended-response question below requires you to think about more than one of the passages you have just read. Read the question carefully and write your answer in the space provided. Use complete sentences, correct punctuation, and proper grammar. Be sure to answer each part of the question.

EXTENDED-RESPONSE QUESTION
THEME 6: ANCIENT ANIMALS

How can people still study and learn about animals that lived on Earth millions of years ago? What can we learn about these animals?

Use details from the passages you have just read to support your answer.

_____

_____

_____

_____

_____

_____

_____

_____

_____

_____

_____

Introduction to Theme 7:

Learning from Each Other

Different people can learn from each other. We can learn from making friends from other countries, visiting other countries, and living and working in other places.

DIRECTIONS: Now you will read three stories. Read and think about each story. Then answer the questions.

Good Readers

Good Readers ask themselves questions about what they are reading and take notes:

_____

_____

_____

_____

_____

_____

_____

_____

_____

_____

_____

_____

Learning from Each Other

Be a Pen Pal!

Join **Pen Pals Around the World** and become a pen pal! It is the best way to make friends around the world.

How to Become a Pen Pal

1. You must be a student in grade 3 through grade 12 to join.

2. Write a letter to your pen pal. For the first letter, you won't know who or where your pen pal is—but that's part of the fun. Be sure to tell your name, your age, and what you like to do.

3. Get an envelope. On the envelope, write your address and put on two stamps. This is the envelope your new friend will use to send a letter back to you. Fold your letter around this envelope and put both into another envelope.

4. On another piece of paper, write this information: your name, age, and address. If you have an e-mail address, write that, too.

5. Mail your letter and the paper with your information to:

Pen Pals Around the World
P.O. Box 444
New York, NY 10000

6. Your letter and information will be sent to a pen pal. Your pen pal will be a student your age who lives in a different country.

7. In seven to eight weeks, you will receive a letter from your pen pal. The two of you can keep writing and stay in touch!

DIRECTIONS: Read each question carefully. Darken the circle for each correct answer. For Question 5, write your answer in the space below the question.

1 **You can tell the person who wrote the flyer thinks that**

Ⓐ letter writing is a good way to make friends

Ⓑ e-mail is better than writing letters

Ⓒ the best friends are usually just like you

Ⓓ talking is easier than writing letters

Why did you choose your answer?

_____

_____

2 **About how old will the student who writes back to you be?**

Ⓐ older than you

Ⓑ younger than you

Ⓒ about your age

Ⓓ the flyer doesn't say

Why did you choose your answer?

_____

_____

3 **What is the *first* thing you will do to become a pen pal?**

Ⓐ get a letter from a pen pal

Ⓑ write a letter to a pen pal

Ⓒ get an envelope

Ⓓ send your letter

> **Why did you choose your answer?**
>
> _____
>
> _____

4 **The information on this flyer was written in order to**

Ⓐ teach you about life in other countries

Ⓑ show you how to write a letter

Ⓒ get you to travel to other places

Ⓓ tell you how to become a pen pal

> **Why did you choose your answer?**
>
> _____
>
> _____

5   **Why do you send your first letter to New York?**

_____

_____

_____

_____

_____

_____

Why do you think this is the answer?

_____

_____

_____

Good Readers ask themselves questions about what they are reading and take notes:

_____

_____

_____

_____

_____

_____

_____

_____

_____

_____

_____

_____

_____

Learning from Each Other

My Year in South Africa

I remember the morning a year ago when my dad came home with the news. "Ashley," he said, "we are going to live in South Africa next year."

I was not excited. My dad is a professor. He teaches at the college near my house. He wanted to live in South Africa to learn more about their government. I wanted to stay at home in Ohio and go to school with my friends. A year living in South Africa sounded like a long time to be away.

When we left Ohio last July, it was summertime. But South Africa is on the opposite side of the equator from Ohio. That meant that it was the middle of winter in South Africa. I wasn't pleased about missing summer.

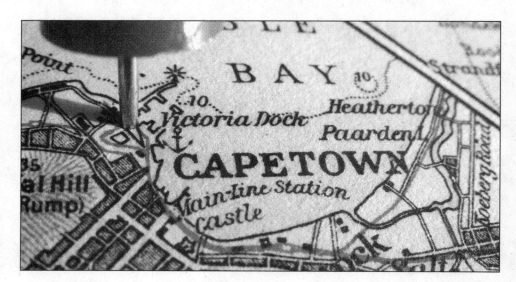

We flew in an airplane to a city called Cape Town. Most people in Cape Town speak English, but the English is different from American English. South Africans call sweaters "jerseys" and they call the mail "the post." People in South Africa speak many other languages, too. To speak some of the African languages, you have to make little clicking sounds in your mouth.

Soon after we got to South Africa, we visited a game park. We saw lions, elephants, gazelles, and giraffes. I learned that giraffes do not make any sounds and that they have purple tongues that are almost one foot long.

After our trip, I started school. My first day at school was difficult, but I learned that people are not so different just because they live in a different place. I made many friends. Someday I hope they visit me in Ohio.

I never thought I would say this when I went on that first trip to South Africa last year, but now I hope that someday I will go to South Africa again.

Good Readers take notes:

_____

_____

_____

_____

_____

_____

DIRECTIONS: Read each question carefully. Darken the circle for each correct answer. For Question 5, write your answer in the space below the question.

1 **How did Ashley feel when she learned she was going to South Africa?**

Ⓐ excited

Ⓑ unhappy

Ⓒ proud

Ⓓ curious

Why did you choose your answer?

_____

_____

_____

2 **Why did Ashley miss summer when she went to South Africa?**

Ⓐ The weather is always hot in South Africa.

Ⓑ The weather is always cold in South Africa.

Ⓒ Ashley had to start school right away in South Africa.

Ⓓ South Africa is on the opposite side of the equator from Ohio.

Why did you choose your answer?

_____

_____

3 **In South African English, a sweater is called**

Ⓐ an eraser

Ⓑ an elephant

Ⓒ the post

Ⓓ a jersey

Why did you choose your answer?

_____

_____

4 **This story is most like a**

Ⓐ mystery

Ⓑ fairy tale

Ⓒ folktale

Ⓓ true story

Why did you choose your answer?

_____

_____

5 **How did Ashley's feelings and thoughts about South Africa change from the time she first went there until the time she came home one year later?**

_____

_____

_____

_____

_____

Why do you think this is the answer?

_____

_____

Good Readers

Good Readers ask themselves questions about what they are reading and take notes:

_____

_____

_____

_____

_____

_____

_____

_____

_____

_____

_____

_____

Learning from Each Other
The Peace Corps

Would you like to travel to faraway lands? Would you like to help people? Would you like to learn more about yourself and other people? A job in the Peace Corps might be in your future.

Every year, thousands of Americans go to live and work in other countries around the world. These Americans work to make life better for the people of these countries. They teach them about health. They teach them new ways to farm and take care of the land around them. They teach children English, math, and science. These Americans are volunteers for the Peace Corps.

The Peace Corps started in 1961 when John F. Kennedy, the President of the United States, worried that people thought about themselves too much. President Kennedy said that Americans should, "Ask not what your country can do for you, ask what you can do for your country." He meant that people should think of ways they could help other people. He started the Peace Corps.

©Ljupco Smokovski/dreamstime.com

The Peace Corps has three goals. The first is to <u>improve</u> the lives of people around the world. Second, the Peace Corps hopes that people in other countries will learn more about Americans. And, last but not least, the Peace Corps hopes that Americans will learn more about other countries and people. By learning more about other people and working together, the Peace Corps promotes world peace and friendship.

Peace Corps volunteers help to make the world a smaller place. They make life better for friends in places around the world. Who knows? Maybe one day you will be a Peace Corps volunteer.

Good Readers take notes:

_____

_____

_____

_____

_____

_____

_____

DIRECTIONS: Read each question carefully. Darken the circle for each correct answer. For Question 5, write your answer in the space below the question.

1 **What is the best summary of this story?**

Ⓐ Thousands of Americans have worked in other countries.

Ⓑ Peace Corps workers make life better for people around the world.

Ⓒ The Peace Corps was started in 1961 by John F. Kennedy.

Ⓓ Someday someone you know might work for the Peace Corps.

Why did you choose your answer?

_____

_____

_____

2 **The ideas in the third paragraph tell about**

Ⓐ how two things are different

Ⓑ how something changed over time

Ⓒ a problem and how it was solved

Ⓓ a main idea and details about it

Why did you choose your answer?

_____

_____

_____

3 **Which of these jobs would *not* be done by someone working for the Peace Corps?**

Ⓐ feeding homeless people in Chicago

Ⓑ teaching math in South America

Ⓒ farming with people in Asia

Ⓓ bringing clean water to a village in Africa

Why did you choose your answer?

_____

_____

_____

4 In this story, to <u>improve</u> means to

Ⓐ keep something the same

Ⓑ take something away

Ⓒ make something worse

Ⓓ make something better

Why did you choose your answer?

_____

_____

5 What does the author of this story mean when she states, "Peace Corps volunteers help to make the world a smaller place"?

_____

_____

_____

_____

_____

Why do you think this is the answer?

_____

_____

Theme Question

DIRECTIONS: The extended-response question below requires you to think about more than one of the passages you have just read. Read the question carefully and write your answer in the space provided. Use complete sentences, correct punctuation, and proper grammar. Be sure to answer each part of the question.

EXTENDED-RESPONSE QUESTION
THEME 7: LEARNING FROM EACH OTHER

Why is it a good idea for people who live in different countries to learn about each other? Explain some different ways in which you could get to know and learn about people from other countries. What might you learn?

Use details from the passages you have just read to support your answer.

_____

_____

_____

_____

_____

_____

_____

_____

_____

_____

_____

_____